Taming the Ox

BOOKS BY CHARLES JOHNSON

FICTION

Bending Time: The Adventures of Emery Jones, Boy Science Wonder
(with Elisheba Johnson, illustrated by Charles Johnson, 2013)
Dr. King's Refrigerator: And Other Bedtime Stories (2005)
Soulcatcher: And Other Stories (2001)
Dreamer (1998)
Middle Passage (1990)
The Sorcerer's Apprentice: Tales and Conjurations (1986)
Oxherding Tale (1982)
Faith and the Good Thing (1974)

PHILOSOPHY

Philosophy: An Innovative Introduction
(with Michael Boylan, 2010)
Being and Race: Black Writing since 1970 (1988)

NONFICTION

Passing the Three Gates: Interviews with Charles Johnson
(edited by Jim McWilliams, 2004)
Turning the Wheel: Essays on Buddhism and Writing (2003)
King: The Photobiography of Martin Luther King, Jr.
(with Bob Adelman, 2000)
I Call Myself an Artist: Writings by and about Charles Johnson
(edited by Rudolph Byrd, 1999)
Africans in America: America's Journey through Slavery
(with Patricia Smith, 1998)
Black Men Speaking (with John McCluskey, Jr., 1997)

DRAWINGS

Half-Past Nation-Time (1972)
Black Humor (1970)

TAMING THE OX

Buddhist Stories and Reflections on Politics,
Race, Culture, and Spiritual Practice

CHARLES JOHNSON

A Work from the Johnson Construction Co.

SHAMBHALA | *Boston & London*

SHAMBHALA PUBLICATIONS, INC.
Horticultural Hall
300 Massachusetts Avenue
Boston, Massachusetts 02115
www.shambhala.com

9 8 7 6 5 4 3 2 1

FIRST EDITION
Printed in the United States of America

∞ This edition is printed on acid-free paper that meets the
American National Standards Institute z39.48 Standard.
♻ This book is printed on 30% postconsumer recycled paper.
For more information please visit www.shambhala.com.
Distributed in the United States by Penguin Random House LLC
and in Canada by Random House of Canada Ltd

Designed by K. E. White

Library of Congress Cataloging-in-Publication Data
Johnson, Charles, 1948–, author.
[Works. Selections]
Taming the ox: Buddhist stories and reflections on politics,
race, culture, and spiritual practice / Charles R. Johnson.
pages   cm
ISBN 978-1-61180-183-5 (paperback)
1. Buddhism—Social aspects. 2. Buddhism and politics. I. Title.
BQ4570.S6J63 2014
294.3'3—dc23
2014008561

Page 193 constitutes a continuation of the copyright page.

For my grandson, Emery Charles Spearman

अक्कोधेन जिने कोधं असाधुं साधुना जिने।
जिने कदरियं दानेन सच्चेनालिक वादिनं ॥

Conquer hate with love,
Evil with good,
Meanness with generosity,
And lies with truth.

  —*Dhammapada*, chapter 17, verse 223

Contents

Part Two: Reviews and Prefaces

Part Three: Stories

Preface

OF ALL THE BOOKS I'VE PUBLISHED, fiction and nonfiction, the most spiritually rewarding work was *Turning the Wheel: Essays on Buddhism and Writing* (2003). On its pages, the two activities that have anchored my life for sixty-five years and reinforce each other—creative production and spiritual practice—were humbly offered to readers as moments that crystallized what I had learned during my passage through American literature, the visual arts, and the Buddhadharma.

But ten years have now passed since that book's publication. And another decade of Buddhist-themed works have been published since the essays collected in *Turning the Wheel*. Other significant changes have taken place as well.

While I am a Western-educated philosopher, artist, and writer, I have to confess that I've always felt very much at home with elements of Far Eastern cultures. Since my teens, the vision of how we should live that impressed me more than any other is captured in what some call the traditional "Four Stages (or Seasons) of Life" in Hindu culture. (For a strict interpretation of this, see the story "Prince of the Ascetics" in this volume.) In youth (spring), we are told, our job is not to play or waste time at frivolous pursuits but simply to study and acquire as many practical skills as possible. Then in young adulthood (summer) we enter the work world with its endless duties and various obligations, and we use those skills and that knowledge to serve others.

In middle age (fall), we devote ourselves to our families and communities as householders, working ceaselessly and with nonattachment, creating various forms of wealth so that we can share its benefits with as many sentient beings as possible while expecting nothing in return. There is an almost ascetic dimension to the daily sacrifice and service of the householder's life, one beautifully disclosed in the often quite humorous Buddhist *Vimalakirti Sutra*. (And humor, believe me, is rare in the sutras.) There, we learn about townsman Vimalakirti, who is not a monk but lives by the guidelines for monks (*vinaya*) as a layperson or *upasaka*.

What I found remarkable about the season of the householder, which I was living thoroughly a decade ago, was that Vimalakirti "observed all the rules of pure conduct laid down for monks, and though he lived at home, he felt no attachment to the threefold world. One could see he had a wife and children, yet he was at all times chaste in action; obviously he had kin and household attendants, yet he always delighted in withdrawing from them. Although he wore jewels and finery, his real adornment was the auspicious marks; although he ate and drank like others, what he truly savored was the joy of meditation."

For the skilled, hardworking householder, then, and unlike the *bhikkhu* who retires to a monastery, the "mud and mire of a damp, low-lying place" is the proper realm for his spiritual practice, though this immersion in the phenomenal world leaves him as unstained as the lotus flower:

He shows himself subject to the five desires
Yet he is also seen to practice meditation.

To live as a lotus among flames—
this may be deemed a rare thing.
To exist amid desire yet practice meditation—
this too is rare!

Vimalakirti the householder enters "the great sea of earthly desires" without dualism, yearning for nothing, loathing nothing; he takes "delight in being friendly with those of like learning" as well as "delight in a mind free of anger and hostility when among those of unlike learning," knowing there is nothing to be practiced, and no one who practices, yet fervently turning the wheel of Dharma just the same.

The householder's life is perhaps the most fascinating of all the seasons. But soon enough there comes the beginning of old age (winter), when the householder retires from the worldliness of the world to devote himself more fully to matters of the spirit, to knowledge (*vidya*) and preparation for his inevitable exit from this existence.

As evidenced by the iron-gray tendrils threading my eyebrows, hair, and beard; by my children now being grown and my beloved parents buried; by my retirement from teaching five years ago after thirty-four years in the classroom (which leaves me with four to five days a week for working out: treadmill for 100 minutes, bench press with weight at 230, and martial-art practice with old friends); by my taking formal vows as a lay Buddhist in the Soto Zen tradition in 2007; and especially by the birth of my grandson Emery Charles Spearman two years ago, I find myself standing with thanksgiving a few steps beyond the fall of the householder and at the mysterious yet attractive onset of winter. Yet an old man playing with his grandson, doing goofy things that make him giggle, seeing things fresh again through the eyes of a child, finds himself happily returned to that state Buddhists call "beginner's mind."

For all these reasons, then, it seems appropriate now for me to assemble a sequel to that first collection of essays. The works that you will find on these pages range over different forms and genres, for the capacious Buddhist experience is simply the human experience in all its colors and complexities. They include not only essays but short stories—set in the East and West, the past and present—that dialogue with the nonfiction here, and also occasional pieces—reviews and prefaces—that address traditional issues related to Buddhism in general and the recent, revolutionary emergence of black American Dharma practice in particular. They originally appeared in publications as diverse as *Tricycle: The Buddhist Review, Shambhala Sun, Turning Wheel: Socially Engaged Buddhism, Buddhadharma: The Practitioner's Quarterly,* the *International Journal of African American Art,* and the *Boston Review.*

My hope is that readers, and one day my grandson, will find on these pages something of the timeless wisdom and beauty that allowed the famous Chinese poet P'ang-yun to look at his journey through life and see the sacred in the secular, Nirvana in Samsara, the transcendent in the everyday, and joyfully proclaim:

How wonderful, how marvelous!!
I fetch wood, I carry water!

Dr. Charles Johnson
Seattle, Washington
April 2014

PART ONE

Essays

1 | The Dharma and the Artist's Eye

TO CONSIDER ONESELF A BUDDHIST, says His Holiness the Dalai Lama, one must embrace the Four Noble Truths expounded two and a half millennia ago by Shakyamuni Buddha during his forty-five years as a teacher of the Dharma. Regardless of one's lineage or tradition, these truths state that (1) there is suffering; (2) the cause of suffering is thirst (*trishna*), which most commentators interpret as being selfish desire; (3) there is a way to end suffering; and (4) that way is the Eightfold Path (*arya astanga marga*). Of the eight steps on this path, the one to which the others build and in which they triumphantly culminate is Right Mindfulness (*samyak smrti*). It is the root and fruit of all Buddhist practice.

As a Buddhist and phenomenologist, I understand at age fifty-eight, and after twenty-six years of practicing meditation, something of the depths of clarity and insight delivered by Right Mindfulness. But it was as a young artist in my teens—someone for whom drawing and encountering art from all cultures, historical periods, and countries had been a passion since childhood—that Eastern philosophies and religions first seduced me. The seeds for my journey to the East were sown when I was fourteen in Evanston, Illinois. I pulled down a volume on yoga from my mother's shelf of books in our living room and, after reading the chapter devoted to "Meditation," I spent the next half an hour in my bedroom following its instructions for vipassana, the method Shakyamuni Buddha recommended for his followers in the magnificent *Mahasatipatthana Sutra* ("The Great Discourse on the Foundations of Mindfulness"). It was the most peaceful and renewing thirty minutes I'd ever known, an experience that radically slowed down my sense of time and cleared away the background noise always on the edge of my consciousness. The risible "monkey mind" described by Vivekananda in *Raja Yoga* was suddenly quieted. I was seeing without judgment. Without judgment, there were no distinctions. Without distinctions, there was no desire. Without desire, there was only clarity and compassion. After meditation, I was suddenly no longer squandering my energies and consciousness by worrying about things in the past that could not be recovered or changed, nor was I preliving a future that would never come. Rather, all my attention rested peacefully in the present moment, a total immersion in the *here* and *now* very similar to the state of self-forgetting artists know well from focused moments of creation. To my astonishment, I felt capable of infinite patience with and empathy for my parents, teachers, and friends. Within me, I detected not the slightest trace of fear or anger or anxiety about anything. Nor was I conscious of myself, only of what was in my field of consciousness, and *that,* of course, was indeed an unusual event in the life of a fourteen-year-old American boy in 1962.

But in addition to being transformative and rewarding that first meditation was frightening, too. I wondered what the hell I'd just done to myself. I felt as if I'd been playing with a loaded pistol, a powerful tool I could not control because at that time I did not have a teacher. So for a long time I backed away from meditation. I feared it might make me too detached and dispassionate and lacking the fire—the desire and internal agitation—for venturing out into the world and exploring all the things, high and low, that I, as a teenager, was burning to see, know, and taste.

Ironically, that very hunger for worldly experience brought me face to face again with the haunting practices I'd been briefly exposed to in the Dharma, for even the briefest glimpse is enough to change one's life and orientation forever. Whenever I encountered anything related to Buddhism or Taoism—a Zen painting like Liu Ts'ai's fourteenth-century *Fishes* memorable for its harmony, restraint, and understatement, or a haiku by Basho so pure in its simplicity that it seemed a thing discovered in Nature—I found myself stopped cold, thrown instantly into an attitude of egoless listening and inner peace as if I'd suddenly heard a call of remembrance to look within myself, my own mind, for the origin of all I experienced, a call that also beckoned me home. This was especially true when, still in my teens, I experienced either desire or anger, for no sooner than those emotions made possible by dualism arose, a partitioning of the world into self and other, I became aware of the contribution of my own conditioned thoughts to the way the thing desired appeared. "Now why," I would wonder, "do I want or believe *that*? Why do I think such a thing will bring me happiness? Am I truly seeing this person or thing or feeling clearly? Through my own eyes or those of my parents, friends, teachers or Madison Avenue? Are these thoughts and judgments my own or have I *received* them from others?" Once I asked those questions, and turned inward to examine the rising and falling of my own thoughts and feelings (which is the essence of vipassana), attachment to and thirst for the thing desired inevitably diminished, and finally disappeared, leaving only aesthetic appreciation for it, and a feeling of thanksgiving.

So wherever I turned in my teens, the Dharma seemed to beckon me. In college, I was a philosophy and journalism major, and a professional cartoonist. I had studied with the cartoonist and writer Lawrence Lariar, starting when I was fifteen, then began publishing catalog illustrations for a Chicago magic company, award-winning cartoons, and comic strips (and also three short stories in my school newspaper) when I was seventeen in 1965. Between that year and 1972, I published over one thousand drawings and illustrations as a political cartoonist, two collections of drawings (*Black Humor* in 1970 and *Half-Past Nation-Time* in 1972), and created, produced, and hosted an early PBS how-to-draw series, *Charlie's Pad* (1970). When not studying for my classes in Western philosophy or working on assignments for publications like the *Chicago Tribune,* the *Southern Illinoisan, Black World* (formerly *Negro Digest*) and *Jet,* I consumed in translation the major texts of first Buddhism, then Hinduism and Taoism (and I now deeply enjoy translating Sanskrit works in the first religion from the original Devanagari texts).

During the racially turbulent late 1960s, when anger and violence, the polarization of blacks and whites, the young and old, was everywhere around me, these works became my spiritual refuge. I remained devoted to researching and writing about African American and African history and culture, of course, and discovered that the study of Eastern philosophies enriched and enabled that lifelong project. I devoured everything in print by D. T. Suzuki, Eugen Herrigel, Christmas Humphreys, Alan Watts, and a library of esoteric books by authors from India, China, and Japan. I took courses on Lao Tzu, Chuang Tzu, and the Vedas. I studied over and over the "Ten Oxherding Pictures" of twelfth-century Zen artist Kakuan Shien (and now use Tomikichiro Tokuriki's woodcut version as the screensaver on my PC) and other Asian artworks as if they were the visual equivalent of a mantra. In Liang K'ai's thirteenth-century sketch *The Sixth Patriarch Tears up a Sutra,* I saw a spontaneity in his brushstrokes that seemed analogous to the sudden, instantaneous experience of satori favored by Ch'an (Zen) Buddhists. In Ma Yüan's *Landscape in Moonlight* (1200 C.E.) and Kao K'o-kung's *Landscape after Rain* (1250–1300 C.E.), my eyes moved over paintings that gently nudged me into seeing how all things from the very first have eternally been in a perfect state of tranquillity. Ephemeral cliffs and mountain peaks were forms briefly manifest from a fecund emptiness (*sunyata*) that, mysteriously, was also a plenitude of being. Such forms arose (trees, clouds, people), were captured on silk, but were ever on the verge of vanishing back into the Undifferentiated, the Non-Dual, leaving no trace of themselves like waves on water. Both works were fine examples of how the "beautiful" was attained in Buddhist art: namely by dissolving the false distinction or duality between the beautiful and the ugly—it was the realm *before* their ontological and epistemological separation (by mind, by language) and obscuring by relativity that I was seeing in Eastern art.

We might also say these images sprang from a transcendent vision identical to the one that infuses Tibetan sand mandalas, the making of which requires years of practice and is a form of meditation through art dating back to the sixth and seventh centuries. Tapping out colored grains of sand from a funnel called a *chakpu*, monks create elaborate, minutely detailed palaces and grounds for Buddhist deities. One tiny lotus may take hours to make. And then, after several days, after the mandala is done, its creators toss the sand into local waters to illustrate the impermanence of all things—even breathtakingly beautiful ones.

However, study alone became inadequate for satisfying my increasing absorption with the practices of Eastern philosophy. I could never shake the nagging sense that the Buddhadharma was something I had to work with more creatively. Specifically, I felt in the late 1960s and early 1970s compelled to come to terms with

Shakyamuni Buddha's phenomenological insight into *ahumkara*, the "I-maker" he unveiled when meditating beneath the bodhi tree; his beautiful description of the impermanence and codependence (*pratitya samutpada*) of all things; the rightness of a life devoted to *ahimsa* ("harmlessness to all sentient beings"); and the very Eastern truth that ontological dualism was one of the profoundest tricks of the mind. I wondered: Was race an illusion, a product of *avidya,* or ignorance? And when Buddhists recited the terse and trenchant Pali formulation *anicca dukkha anatta* ("Everything is transitory and impermanent, *anicca;* there is universal suffering, *dukkha;* and there is no self, *anatta*"), what did this ancient wisdom, especially the denial of an enduring, essential self, imply for Westerners in general and black Americans in particular?

Inevitably, then, I turned from my early career as a cartoonist to writing the Buddhist- and Taoist- and Vedanta-themed novels *Oxherding Tale* and *Middle Passage*, short stories like "China" and "Kwoon," and essays such as "The Elusive Art of Mindfulness" to more fully explore and dramatize these provocative questions. And, yes, I finally found the meditation teachers I needed and began daily practice in earnest in 1981, no longer fearing where a publicly declared devotion to Buddhism would take me—indeed, knowing at that juncture in my life that however small and insignificant might be my "turning the wheel of Dharma," this was crucial for my very survival as a "black" artist, college professor, writer, father, son, husband, colleague, and friend in a society that was growing more and more spiritually bankrupt, culturally provincial, ideologically balkanized, yet very Eurocentric as it entered deeper into a demonstrable period of late decadence. For to practice this way of life is to live without a safety net; to be open to all views and experiences; to be a verb and not a noun; to no longer "stick" to anything; and, as the bodhisattva ideal and Metta Bhavana *gatha* ("loving-kindness prayer") of Mahayana Buddhism urge us, to spend one's days energetically as an *upasaka* (lay Buddhist follower) working from our various stations in life to reduce the suffering of all sentient beings and assist them in their journey to awakening.

All forms of art play a role in that spiritual project. But whatever means are employed—sketch, painting, or sculpture—creativity influenced by Buddhism or Taoism captures what the Japanese call *myo*, the spiritual, inner radiance of the beautiful. "Human eyes," Wang Wei wrote in the fifth century, "are limited in their scope. Hence they are not able to perceive all that is to be seen; yet with one small brush I can draw the vast universe." Reflecting on this approach, art historian E. H. Gombrich wrote in *The Story of Art* that Chinese artists "paint water and mountains in a spirit of reverence, not in order to teach any particular lesson, nor merely as decorations, but to provide material for deep thought. Their pictures on silk scrolls were kept in precious containers and only unrolled in quiet moments, to be looked at and pondered over as one might open a book of poetry and re-read a beautiful verse."

In other words, for both artist and audience, the artwork and its process of creation presented the occasion for meditation leading to awakening. That, in part, is my understanding of the simultaneously mystical and practical Japanese Zen Buddhist term *wabi sabi*—that is, art that provides a direct, intuitive in-sight into truth. Far different from Western theories of the beau-tiful derived from Greeks' notions, in *wabi* (things fresh, simple, and quiet) *sabi* (things radiating beauty with age), which covers arts as diverse as Zen gardens, flower arrangement, the tea cere-mony, poetry, and the music played by wandering monks (*hon-kyoku*), we find a preference for such features as imperfection, impermanence, immediacy, the idiosyncratic, incompleteness, modesty, and humility.

Originally *wabi* literally meant "poverty"—for example, that of hermits. From an initial negative denotation it came to imply freedom and nondependence on possessions and all the trappings of a materialistic society. Aesthetically, it is the perfect realization of Right Mindfulness, as described by Bhikkhu Bodhi—not a process of heaping up or accumulating things and ideas, but rather one of "letting go," being "a matter not so much of doing but of undoing, not thinking, not judging, not associating, not planning, not imagining, not wishing."

And it is through the everydayness of such an (un)remarkable art that we are blessed to experience the ordinary mind as a portal to transcendence and liberation.

2 | Dharma for a Dangerous Time

The painfully perturbing dissolution of familiar forms, which suggests to weaker spirits that the ultimate reality is nothing but a chaos, may reveal to a steadier and more spiritual vision the truth that the flickering film of the phenomenal world is an illusion which cannot obscure the eternal unity that lies behind it.
—Arnold J. Toynbee, *A Study of History*

FOR THOSE WHO TAKE REFUGE IN THE teachings of the Dharma, a crucial and recurring theme in our meditation is the experience of impermanence (*anicca*) and the inevitability of change. For a decade now, I've occasionally tried out on my friends and students a prediction about this historical moment we find ourselves living through at the dawn of the twenty-first century. It's an idea about change for which I have only anecdotal examples, and no empirical proof whatsoever, which means this conjecture is only a hunch at best, something glimpsed furtively in one's peripheral vision, but perhaps it might serve as a useful thought experiment when the changes, local and global, reshaping our world so rapidly cause us to feel anxiety, fear, or anger.

For me, it is axiomatic that while pain is inevitable in life, suffering is produced by the mind, frequently by our conditioned ideas of what is and ought to be. I find it helpful to remember that in the 4.5-billion-year history of the earth, modern humans (one of twenty humanoid species that once existed) have only been around for an estimated 100,000 years, the mere blink of an eye in a universe 13.7 billion years old. Furthermore, 23.3 percent of that universe consists of dark matter, and 72.1 percent of dark energy, which leaves the measurable cosmos—what we can experience—at only about 4.6 percent. During our brief, flicker-flash time here, there have been long periods of stagnation in our social evolution, notably the Dark and Middle Ages, which lasted a thousand years. But since the seventeenth century of Descartes, and certainly since the European Enlightenment, civilizational change has seemed relatively constant, and even sometimes marked by brief, intense periods that compress paradigm shifts and technological developments so far-reaching one is tempted to compare them to the movement of tectonic plates that alter continents and reshape the surface of the earth. Old and often cherished ideas and ways of life die; new experiences arise and require a new vocabulary, a new grammar, a new vision.

For example, a glance at the thirty years between 1895 and 1925 discloses a startling shift from the horse-and-carriage world of my great-grandparents (who lived a hairsbreadth from slavery and when average life expectancy was forty-seven years in 1902) to one in which the era of the Victorians ended, quantum mechanics provided a deeper understanding of matter than had classical or Newtonian physics, new forms of art emerged (poetry's free-verse movement, the revolt against formalism, the paintings of Picasso, and the sculpture of Eric Gill), and new philosophical and conceptual models took hold. In a very short time, our lives filled with the all-too-familiar "furniture" of the twentieth century. In just three dizzying decades, such forms as the airplane, radio, modern naval submarine, diesel engine, typewriter, electric iron, talking pictures, television, X-rays, zippers, and the calculating machine all came into being and restructured the possibilities of lived experience.

However, even that period of accelerated change, of the rise and fall of phenomena, seems lethargic when compared to the florescent moment we find ourselves immersed in at the beginning of a new century (and millennium). Given the sequencing of DNA, and the exponential progress in such fields as biotechnology, robotics, and nanotechnology, our children may live in a world as experientially different from the twentieth century as our time is from, say, the eighteenth. As a species, we have sent probes to Mars, Venus, and the comet Tempel 1 and to objects in the outer solar system like Saturn's moon Titan—all with the aim of clarifying the origins of our universe and delivering knowledge unknown to our predecessors. "Chimeras," creatures genetically engineered with the traits of two species—fluorescent animals, for example—are already among us. Scientists have achieved "quantum teleportation," the transfer of physical characteristics between atoms. A time may come, and soon, when stem cell research allows us to grow livers and kidneys keyed to our individual DNA, thus removing the likelihood of such organs being rejected by our immune systems. "People have this sense that as twenty-first century humans we've gotten as high as we're going to go," says Greg Wray, director for studies of evolutionary genomics at Duke University. "But we're not played out as a species. We're still evolving."

Yet that evolution, of course, is contingent on whether we as a species can survive. Martin Luther King Jr. observed in a sermon delivered in 1954 that "the great problem facing modern man is that the means *by* which we live have outdistanced the spiritual ends *for* which we live. . . . The real problem is that through our scientific genius we've made of the world a neighborhood, but through our moral and spiritual genius we've failed to make it a brotherhood."

How remarkable it is that half a century after King delivered that speech our era looks eerily like the time of Petronius, author of the *Satyricon* at the end of the Roman empire.

On the global level, we often feel that we are helpless spectators to a war on terrorism that the vice president of the United States warned will continue well into the next generation. The Iraq war, now three years old, with its "thousands" of strategic errors Secretary of State Condoleeza Rice confesses the United States has made (which include, many would say, invading that country after cherry-picking basically flawed intelligence), leaves Americans of conscience and goodwill in a daily state of anxiety and suspense greater than any novelist can achieve, hoping that a sectarian civil war between Sunnis, Shiites, and Kurds can be avoided, and that the Middle East will not be further destabilized by the dream of jihadists spread across eighty countries: namely, a modern holy war between Muslims and Christians (and Jews). As I have followed the unfolding events in dangerous neighborhoods like Iraq and Afghanistan, I have been shocked and sickened by the almost surrealistic images of prisoners humiliated at Abu Ghraib, by the videotaped decapitation of American business-man Nicholas Berg in Iraq by the al-Qaida militant Abu Musab-al-Zarqawi, by the seemingly endless suicide and car bombings, by the kidnappings and torture of innocents, by the deaths and mutilations of between thirty thousand and one hundred thou-sand Iraqis, as well as over two thousand Americans and coalition forces (and still counting). Even Stephen King's feverish imagina-tion doesn't compare to *this* real-world horror story.

Across the border from Iraq, Iranian President Mahmoud Ahmadinejad questions the abundantly documented reality of the Holocaust, promises in his speeches that the state of Israel must be "wiped off the map," and works with his nation's mullahs toward the production of enriched uranium that could be used to make a nuclear bomb. In the first letter to an American president from an Iranian leader since 1979, Ahmadinejad attacked the fundamental values of the West, stating in May that liberalism and Western-style democracy "have not been able to realize the ideals of humanity. . . . Today these two concepts have failed. Those with insight can already hear the sounds of the shattering and fall of the ideology and thoughts of the Liberal democratic systems."

Meanwhile, in Sudan's Darfur region, where an Arab militia called the Janjaweed has raped, killed, and driven ethnic African villagers from their homes in the past three years, twenty thousand people have died. The United Nations calls this "one of the world's worst humanitarian disasters." (Given so much admirable work done by the United Nations, I would rather not dwell on distasteful reports of its peacekeepers, aid workers, and teachers trading money and food for sex with African girls as young as eight years old.)

And here in America, a plutocracy with a broken moral compass, a cook's tour of our dilemmas reveals that our ship of state has run aground on the problems of immigration, poverty, the lack of universal health care, the complex issue of a planet-altering global warming, political corruption such as influence peddling by lobbyists like Jack Abramoff, the aftermath of Hurricane Katrina, racism, the startling decline of literacy (Only 31 percent of college graduates can read a complex book and extrapolate from it), the loss of not only civility and courtesy but also safety in so many of our public spaces, the failure of 1,750 schools to meet the No Child Left Behind standards for math and reading (all fifty states received an F from the federal government on demonstrating their teachers had a bachelor's degree, a state license, and proven competency in every subject they teach), a burgeoning prison industry, the failure to address the plight of young black males from violent, drug-ridden neighborhoods who are increasingly alienated from society, the outsourcing of jobs, growing electronic surveillance and accumulation of private information on citizens, a president (and Congress) with the lowest approval ratings since Richard Nixon, and the saddling of future generations with a staggering national debt. The list of dysteleological characteristics—all signs of internal social decay and decline in what historian Oswald Spengler described in *The Decline of the West* as a culture's period of senility—goes on and on.

Looking at such a pain-wracked world of Samsara where many residents in non-Western nations live on a dollar a day (or less) while materialistic Americans recklessly consume the lion's share of the earth's resources for their entertainment and ease, one justifiably feels despair and a powerlessness to alleviate one's own pain, let alone that of others. Some cultural commentators recommend that we simply withdraw from those dimensions of the world that have become unworkable. I'm thinking of a beautiful Modern Library edition of Voltaire's *Candide* that bears a blurb by the esteemed philosopher A. J. Ayer, who says, "When we observe such things as the recrudescence of fundamentalism in the United States, the horrors of religious fanaticism in the Middle East, the appalling danger which the stubbornness of political intolerance presents to the whole world, we must surely conclude that we can still profit by the example of lucidity, the intellectual honesty and the moral courage of Voltaire." And what wisdom does Voltaire's 1759 classic offer us? The story's final eight lines reveal a psychological strategy popular among many in our troubled time (as well as a surprisingly karmic understanding of cause and effect):

Pangloss sometimes said to Candide: "All events are linked up in this best of all possible worlds; for, if you had not been expelled from the noble castle, by hard kicks in your backside for love of Mademoiselle Cunégonde, if you had not been clapped into the Inquisition, if you had not wandered about America on foot, if you had not stuck your sword in the Baron, if you had not lost all your sheep from the land of Eldorado, you would not be eating candied citrons and pistachios here."

"'Tis well said," replied Candide, "but we must cultivate our gardens."

Living scarred and scared, stressed and depressed, burned out on Utopian thinking, many citizens have turned to tending to their own personal gardens, cocooning with their immediate family and friends, and retreating with a feeling of disillusionment and defeat from efforts to tackle social problems (in other words, "dropping out") as their existential default position. Unlike the era of leaders like Martin Luther King Jr. and Eugene McCarthy, in our period of postmodernism, the belief in a historical and progressive Grand Narrative has been lost.

A more positive spin on the Voltairean solution, one that inches closer to a Buddhist approach, can be found in Morris Berman's powerful *The Twilight of American Culture* (2000), a work the author says he created as "a kind of guidebook for disaffected Americans who feel increasingly unable to fit into this society, and who also feel that the culture has to change if it is to survive." Berman, the author of *Dark Ages America*, is an admirer of Ray Bradbury's inspiring and influential *Fahrenheit 451*, a novel that imagines a coterie of cultural rebels in a book-destroying future dystopia who each memorize a classic work of literature and thus become living books themselves in order to transmit the hard-won treasures of civilization to the next generation.

Today we must do something similar to this, Berman argues, becoming what he calls New Monastic Individuals (NMIs), "a sacred/secular humanist dedicated not to slogans or the fashionable patois of postmodernism, but to Enlightenment values that lie at the heart of our civilization: the disinterested pursuit of truth, the cultivation of art, the commitment to critical thinking inter alia."

Not retreating from an infantilized, culturally diminished social world, where consumers are bombarded with three thousand product messages a day (according to Brad Adgate, senior vice president of the New York branding firm Horizon Media), Berman comments that the NMI

> knows the difference between quality and kitsch, and he seeks to preserve the former in the teeth of a culture that is drowning in the latter. If she is a high school teacher, she has her class read the *Odyssey*, despite the fact that half the teachers in the school have assigned Danielle Steel. If he is a writer, he writes for posterity, not for the best-seller lists. As a mother, she takes her kids camping or to art museums, not *Pocahontas*. He elects, in short, to save his life via the monastic option.

Both the "cultivate your own garden" and NMI models for dealing with no-longer-healthy societies have value, but they are missing the profound clarity provided for twenty-six hundred years by the Buddhadharma, which has witnessed and survived the waxing and waning of civilizations. Albert Einstein is reported to have claimed that "if there is any religion that could cope with modern scientific needs, it would be Buddhism." That quote may be apocryphal, but if the attribution is accurate, Einstein may have been inspired in part by these memorable lines that conclude *The Diamond Sutra:*

Thus shall ye think of all this fleeting world:
A star at dawn, a bubble in a stream;
A flash of lightning in a summer cloud,
A flickering lamp, a phantom, and a dream.

After looking outward, a Buddhist is compelled to look within, and through meditation recognizes the truth of the ephemerality, the arising and falling, of all labile phenomena, whether that be our thoughts and feelings, nations, or situations we judge from our relative perspectives to be "good" or "bad." From the moment of our birth we have been dying, and one day this universe itself will experience proton death. Black holes will eventually evaporate into photons, leaving only a Void from which (perhaps) another, different universe will arise. All that men and women have done will be as if it never was. There is nothing to which we can cling or be attached, including our passionately held "views" on matters political, scientific, or spiritual. Even Buddhism—especially Buddhism—knows it is subject to change. Instead, what is required of us, first and foremost, is what I call "epistemological humility" and an egoless listening to all that is around us. The historian Arnold J. Toynbee recognized this in 1947, and in a remarkably Eastern way, when he wrote in *A Study of History*,

> The music that the rhythm of Yin and Yang beats out is the song of creation; and we shall not be misled into fancying ourselves mistaken because, as we give ear, we can catch the note of creation alternating with the note of destruction. . . . If we listen well we shall perceive that, when the two notes collide, they produce not a discord but a harmony. Creation would not be creative if it did not swallow up all things in itself, including its own opposite.

That region in which a *dhammin dhammiko* (Dharma practitioner) dwells is, therefore, beyond the countless illusory forms
of dualism—Christian and Muslim, spiritual and secular, East
and West, Democrat and Republican, liberal and conservative,
black and white, male and female, life and death—that in the
saha-world, the realm of desire (or *kamadhatu*), we moment by
moment impose upon our experience, thereby obscuring it. We
are all these opposites. And none of them. Recognizing this, a
young Thich Nhat Hanh and his fellow monks during the Vietnam War were empowered to selflessly come to the aid of the
wounded, women and children on both sides of the civil strife
that overwhelmed their country. They chose not to merely tend
their gardens or remain in the monastery memorizing beautiful
sutras, but put the Dharma in practice, *here* and *now*, by allevi-
ating the suffering of sentient beings regardless of their politics,
their past, or their deeds. Clearly, they understood Shakyamuni
Buddha's counsel that we must "Give up what is behind. Give up
what is before. Give up what is in the middle. Cross to the other
shore."

Those words refer, of course, to the movement from delusion
and ignorance to awakening. But, as with all things in the poly-
valent Dharma, they provide us with *upaya kaushala* ("skillful
means") when we feel "unable to fit into this society" and feel that
"the culture must change." Indeed, it must. And like all impermanent things, it will, whether we want it to or not. The point is
that we must always first examine ourselves. When he feels anger
or fear, a Buddhist rightly asks, "*Who* feels this anger and fear?
What is this *I* that knows despair and depression?" (Hunting for
the self, one soon discovers, is as futile as searching for weapons
of mass destruction in Iraq.) During periods of great transition,
like this moment in history, we cannot afford to be trapped and
limited by our own narratives, by a miscellaneous list of egoistic

"likes" and "dislikes," or by the forever running magic show that is a product of the conditioned monkey mind. All that we must give up. As Thich Nhat Hanh and his disciple Claude AnShin Thomas teach endlessly and so beautifully, if we want peace, we must *be* peace ourselves. When I wonder how to achieve Right Speech, I try to remember one of my favorite Zen sayings, "Open mouth, already big mistake," and frisk my planned utterance at Three Gates before I release it into the world. Those Three Gates are questions: Is it true? Is it necessary? Will it do no harm?

Like Right Speech guided by nonviolence and *ahimsa* ("harm-lessness"), Right Action necessarily demands that our deeds do not contribute to division and divisiveness in the world. Leaving our private gardens, we go to *our* workplace, the professional and service organizations we belong to, and other places in the social world where we work in concert with other men and women on life-enhancing, *dukkha*-reducing projects too great for us to accomplish individually. Such work is done with no thought of reward. If we feel we have achieved "merit" through such action, we—inspired by the bodhisattva ideal—might transfer in our practice that "good" karma to other sentient beings for their benefit and happiness, seeking nothing for ourselves, for when we progress enough along the path we no longer create for ourselves the dualism involved in either "good" or "bad" merit. And, once done, we "let go" that particular project and move on to the next, understanding that everything in life—each precious moment—is an opportunity for spiritual practice and not to be wasted by a lack of mindfulness, living always in the present moment (for where else is there to live?), not becoming "stuck" on results, nor to "hope" or "despair," those false polarities that are more about the needs of the fictitious ego, so full of itself, than anything else.

For when we hope we pre-live or project an imagined future spun from our conditioned desires and fears. Hope is baggage we no longer need to carry into this stormy new century once we "cross to the other shore." Hope is thirst (*trishna*), the cause of suffering identified in the Second Noble Truth. Hope raises the question and, as every practitioner knows, hankering for the experience of Nirvana—enlightenment and liberation—is a major impediment on the path, an obstacle to addressing the real, quotidian demands of the *here,* the *now.* If we are not monks but lay Buddhists, *upasakas* and *upasikas*, we must work and practice daily at the white-hot center of Samsara with a glorious hopelessness and devotion to the ten *paramitas* (virtues): loving-kindness (*metta*), compassion (*karuna*), joy in the happiness of others (*mudita*), equanimity (*upekkha*), giving (*dana*), keeping precepts (*shila*), forbearance (*kshanti*), assiduousness (*virya*), meditation (*dhaya*), and wisdom (*prajna*). The *paramitas* vouchsafe no guarantees. They offer no safety net. But for followers of the Dharma, this exhilarating challenge, during the Buddha's time or in our own era of complex and tempestuous change, has always been quite enough.

3 | The Dharma of Social Transformation

Always care compassionately for
The sick, the unprotected, those stricken
With suffering, the lowly and the poor
And take special care to nourish them.
  —Nagarjuna, *The Precious Garland*

WHENEVER I'M ASKED IF THE DHARMA makes possible social
transformations relevant for the specific and seemingly endless
problems of the world today (and I'm asked this often), I find
myself considering that question in light of a provocative critique made forty years ago by Paul Tillich, the great Christian
theologian, who called Buddhism "one of the greatest, strangest, and at the same time most competitive of the religions
proper." In 1963, Tillich published *Christianity and the Encoun-
ter of World Religions,* a series of lectures he gave one year after
his return from a nine-week lecture tour in Japan in 1960. In
his third chapter, "A Christian-Buddhist Conversation," Tillich
takes up the social and ethical consequences, as he sees them,
of his religion in contrast to the Buddhadharma. Of his faith,

he states that a Christian's dedication to the passages in the New Testament that describe *agape*—an unconditional love for others—translates into an energetic form of the social gospel that emphasizes "the *will* to transform individual as well as social structures."

"The Kingdom of God has a revolutionary character," wrote Tillich.

> Christianity . . . shows a revolutionary force directed toward a radical transformation of society. . . . Most of the revolutionary movements in the West—liberalism, democracy, and socialism— are dependent on it, whether they know it or not. There is no analogy to this in Buddhism. Not transformation of reality but salvation from reality is the basic attitude. . . . No belief in the new in history, no impulse for transforming society, can be derived from the principle of Nirvana.

He quickly concedes that a conquering, self-confident will may be problematic because it "leads to the attitude of technical control of nature which dominates the Western world." But, for Tillich, while Buddhism's version of *agape*—*metta* toward all sentient beings—can lead to identification with the other, and thus to empathy, nevertheless "something is lacking: the will to transform the other one either directly or indirectly by transforming the sociological and psychological structures by which he is conditioned."

It is here that the dialogue between Buddhists and Christians (and possibly some social activists) reaches for Tillich a "preliminary end."

At the end of his chapter, Tillich imagines this exchange between a Buddhist priest and a Christian philosopher:

The Buddhist priest asks the Christian philosopher: "Do you believe that every person has a substance of his own which gives
him true individuality?" The Christian answers, "Certainly!" The
Buddhist priest asks, "Do you believe that community between
individuals is possible?" The Christian answers affirmatively. Then
the Buddhist says, "Your two answers are incompatible; if every
person has a substance, no community is possible." To which the
Christian replies, "Only if each person has a substance of his own
is community possible, for community presupposes separation.
You, Buddhist friend, have identity, but not community."

Masao Abe, the distinguished Zen teacher, praised Tillich for
being "the first great Christian theologian in history who tried
to carry out a serious confrontation between Christianity and
Buddhism in their depths." Tillich's influence on spirituality in
America is wide and deep, and inspired the philosophy of Martin
Luther King Jr., who based his goal of achieving the "beloved
community" on the concept of *agape* and devoted his dissertation
at Boston University to Tillich ("A Comparison of the Conceptions of God in the Thinking of Paul Tillich and Henry Nelson
Weiman").

To my eyes, Tillich's assessment of the social and political
shortcomings of Buddhism leaves a good deal to be desired,
especially since it does not account for "engaged Buddhism"
that emerges in the 1960s. Regardless, his sincere misgivings are
shared by many non-Buddhists as well as some new members of
the American convert community struggling to integrate their
practice with a contemporary need for political activism, which
for over two millennia *bhikkhus* judiciously separated from the
Buddhadharma. As students of the Dharma, we should be able
to clarify his questions—the relationship between Nirvana and

our political commitments, and how *anatta* (No-self) fits with a sense of community—through our mindfulness of how key figures and principles in the history and doctrines of Buddhism anticipate and resolve the question, "Is a will toward social transformation lacking in traditional Buddhism?"

For one answer, we need only look to the remarkable life and works of Ashoka, ruler of the Maurya kingdom in 272–236 B.C.E. After waging but one military campaign, which conquered the Kalingas around 264 B.C.E. (150,000 were deported, 100,000 were killed, and many more died), Ashoka was so appalled by the carnage and cruelty of war that he embraced the Dharma and for twenty-eight years devoted himself to the creation of hospitals, charities, public gardens, education for women, the protection of animals, and caring for everyone in his kingdom. He exercised compassion toward lawbreakers and prisoners, cultivated harmonious relations with neighboring states, and encouraged the study of other religions.

The wise *upasaka* Ashoka was hardly alone among leaders who translated the virtue of *ahimsa* ("harmlessness") into civic life. In his book *Inner Revolution*, Robert Thurman reminds us that Nagarjuna was the mentor of King Udayi Shatavahana, sometime between the first century B.C.E. and the second century C.E., and told him, "O King! Just as you love to consider what to do to help yourself, so should you love to consider what to do to help others!"

According to Thurman, Nagarjuna, whose counsel is recorded in the five hundred verses of *The Precious Garland,*

> taught his friend the king how to care for every being in the kingdom: by building schools everywhere and endowing honest, kind, and brilliant teachers; by providing for all his subjects' needs, opening free restaurants and inns for travelers; by

tempering justice with mercy, sending barbers, doctors, and teachers to the prisons to serve the inmates; by thinking of each prisoner as his own wayward child, to be corrected in order to return to free society and use his or her precious human life to attain enlightenment.

Thurman observes, "This activism is implicit in the earliest teachings of the Buddha, and in his actions, though his focus at that time was on individual transformation, the prerequisite of social transformation."

Buddhist history, which Tillich may not have been well acquainted with, offers us time and again concrete examples of how the Dharma has inspired enlightened social policies. But, like many Western intellectuals, Tillich is unable—or perhaps unwilling—to accept the doctrine of *anatta*, and worries a bit more than he should about defining Nirvana. Yet we cannot dismiss too quickly his pivotal question, his most profound challenge to the Dharma: "Do you believe that every person has a substance of his own which gives him true individuality?" In other words, a discrete ego that is enduring, immutable, and independent from other essences.

Clearly, asking this question from the standpoint of Nirvana is as nonsensical as asking, "What is the distance from one o'clock to London Bridge?" Ultimate truth (*paramārtha-satya*) is a nonconceptual and nondiscursive insight into ourselves and the world. Nirvana literally means "to blow out" (*nir,* "out"; *vāna,* "blow") craving and a chimerical sense of the self, like a candle's flame, thereby leading to our experience of things in their true impermanence, codependency, and emptiness (*sunyata*). "In Buddhism," Thich Nhat Hanh reminds us, "we never talk about Nirvana, because Nirvana means the extinction of all notions, concepts, and speech."

However, Buddhism also acknowledges a region of conventional, relative truth (*samvrti-satya*) that is our daily, lived experience, and for this reason Shakyamuni in the sutras can refer to his disciples individually and by name. Here, in the realm of relative truth and contingency, of conditioned arising, each person presents to us a phenomenal, historical "substance," which due to custom and habit we refer to as "individuality." Clearly, since our birth, the *same* things have not happened to or shaped us all. Our lives differ so radically and with such richness that, personally, I prefer to see the Other as a great and glorious mystery about whom I can never make any ironclad assumptions or judgments. The very act of predication is always risky, based on partial information subject to change when new evidence arises.

Thus, what is required of us in the social world is nothing less than vigilant mindfulness. Even though we can say that each person has a "separate" history, the Dharma teaches—as does quantum mechanics—that we are really a process, not a product. An "individuality" ever arising and passing away. A "network of mutuality," each and every one of us, as Martin Luther King Jr. famously said. In the ontology of the Buddhadharma, everything is a shifting assemblage of five skandhas, with no "essence" or "substance" discernible in the concatenation of causes and conditions that create our being instant by instant. For this reason, if I am practicing mindfulness, phenomena ever radiate a surprising and refreshing newness. The "cold" and "wetness" of the water I drank at noon can never be the same "cold" and "wetness" of the water I drink at night. My wife of thirty-six years is hardly—as she will quickly tell you—the same young woman I wooed when we were both twenty years old. (Nor am I the same naïve young swain I was back then, thank heaven!) Far from being "salvation from reality," as Tillich stated, Buddhist meditation is instead a paying of extraordinarily close attention *to* every nuance of our experience.

Something I find worthy of meditation is how in the dialectic between Samsara and Nirvana, the dreamworld of Samsara is logically prior to and quite necessary for the awakening to Nirvana. When discussing Tantric Buddhism, Gunapala Dharmasiri says in the spirit of Nagarjuna, "We make a Samsara out of Nirvana through our conceptual projections. Tantrics maintain that the world is there for two purposes. One is to help us to attain enlightenment. As the world is, in fact, Nirvana, the means of the world can be utilized to realize Nirvana, when used in the correct way."

Perhaps a more concrete way of expressing this in terms of social action is to say we come to the Buddhadharma precisely because the suffering we have experienced in the world of relativity forces us to relentlessly question "conventional" truth and the status quo, as Ashoka discovered that his slaughter of the Kalingas brought him no happiness, or as Buddhist monk Claude AnShin Thomas realized after his killing civilians during the Vietnam War. Or we can consider the case of a black American born in the late 1940s, as I was, a person who knows firsthand the reality of racial segregation in the South and North fifty years ago, and the subtler forms of discrimination in the post–civil rights period, which I call "Jim Crow lite." He (or she) discovers that many Eurocentric whites project fictitious racial "substance" (or meaning) onto people of color, never seeing the mutable individual before them. (Just as unenlightened men do with women.) In their thinking, they dualistically carve the world up in terms of the illusory constructs of "whiteness" and "blackness" and, on the basis of this mental projection, create social structures—as Tillich declared—that fuel attachment, clinging, prejudice, and what the Dharma describes as the "three poisons" of ignorance, hatred, and greed. A black poet expressed powerfully his pain at this reality when he wrote,

"Must I shoot the white man dead / To kill the nigger in his head?"

Fortunately, a black American exposed to the Buddha-dharma sees that these racial illusions so much a part of conventional reality—as the caste system was in the time of the Buddha, who rejected the essentialistic thought that made some men and women "Untouchable"—are products of the relative, conditioned mind. He realizes that while he is not *blind* to what his own valuable yet adventitious racial, gender, or class differences reveal to him, neither is he *bound* by them; and those very phenomenal conditions may, in fact, spark his dedication to social transformations intended to help all sentient beings achieve liberation. The Buddha employed *upaya kaushala* ("skillful means") when he taught the truth of *anatta,* and said he would teach a doctrine *of* self if his followers became attached to the idea of No-self. Always, his teachings foreground the importance of a radical freedom.

Because, as the first line of the *Dhammapada* says, "All that we are is the result of what we have thought," the transformation of "sociological and psychological structures" must take place initially in our own minds—and those of others—if we truly hope to address the root cause of social suffering. Therefore, the Four Noble Truths, the Five Precepts observed by laity and monks alike, the Eightfold Path, and the ten *paramitas* ("perfections") are time-honored blueprints for revolutionary change in, first, the individual, then the community of which he (or she) is a part.

We must, I believe, agree with Tillich when he proclaims that Buddhism is one of the "most competitive religions proper." Without reliance on a higher power, it is competitive exactly to the degree that it is *non*competitive and nondualistic, an orientation toward life that avoids the divisions and divisiveness that are the primary causes of our social problems. This rare quality, in addition to an answer for how relative individuality can be reconciled with our Nirvanic "original face," is beautifully present in a biographical detail from the life of Hui-neng, the Sixth Patriarch of Zen. When he presented himself to the abbot of Tung-shan Monastery in the Huang-mei district of Ch'i-chou in hopes of study, Hui-neng portrayed himself as a poor "commoner from Hsin-chou of Kwangtung."

The abbot rebuked him:

"You are a native of Kwangtung, a barbarian? How can you expect to be a Buddha?"

"Although there are northern men and southern men, north and south make no difference to their Buddha-nature," replied Hui-neng. "A barbarian is different from Your Holiness physically, but there is no difference in our Buddha-nature."

4 | Be Peace Embodied

Do not split the great emptiness into "this" and "that."
—Jifu, seventeenth-century Buddhist nun

DURING THIS PRESIDENTIAL ELECTION year [2004], which many political commentators tell us may prove to be one of the most polarizing, divisive, and rancorous in American (and world) history, followers of the Buddhist Dharma will, like all citizens, be faced with what philosopher Jean-Paul Sartre once called "the agony of choice." To my eye, this is the most glorious of civilization's regular trials, one that defines the nature of a democratic republic. For when the framers of the Constitution declared that the nation's president "shall hold his Office during the term of four years" (Article II, Section 1), they ingeniously guaranteed that a healthy degree of quadrennial change, suspense, tumult, renewal, and spirited debate would be inscribed into our political and social lives. Put another way, American voters, if they take their civic duty seriously, can never rest. Every four years they must decide on the direction of their collective destiny. Twenty-five times in each century they must define for themselves their understanding of the "good life" and vote for candidates and proposals that embody their vision of what this country and its influence should be.

Yet, for all its virtues, this necessary process, which the media frequently presents as a highly competitive "battle" or a "war," can fuel the ugliest partisan passions, fears, frustrations, incivility, and forms of dualism we are likely to find in the realm of Samsara. If perceived through the distorting lens of conflict-laden language and concepts that deliberately pit one citizen against another ("Speech has something in it like a spider's web," Thomas Hobbes once remarked), politics divides people on election night into "winners" and "losers," and creates bitterness and attachment—"dust" is one of the favorite metaphors for this used by followers of the Dharma—that can cloud consciousness and cripple spiritual development, though one of our greatest American leaders, Dr. Martin Luther King Jr., proved time and again that this need not be so.

On December 20, 1956, the day the Montgomery bus boycott ended, King—whose model for nonviolent civil disobedience in Alabama drew inspiration from Mohandas Gandhi's struggle with the British—said, "We must seek an integration based on mutual respect. As we go back to the buses, let us be loving enough to turn an enemy into a friend." Though his home was bombed and his wife and baby endangered during the campaign to end segregation in the "Cradle of the Confederacy," the twenty-six-year-old King never forgot that "all life is interrelated," nor that we are all "caught in an inescapable network of mutuality, tied in a single garment of destiny. Whatever affects one directly, affects all indirectly" in what he called the "beloved community," which in my view is simply the Sangha by another name.

If we can, through the kind of mindfulness often exhibited by Dr. King during one of the most revolutionary moments in American history, remember that politics is merely the skin of social life beneath which we find a more profound experience of ourselves and others, then our Constitution-mandated sea change every four years can potentially be an uplifting experience rather than a spiritually debilitating one. For as the Buddhist nun Jingnuo wrote four centuries ago, "If you bring to everything an illumined mind, you won't get lost."

The Buddhadharma captures such course-correcting illumination in the terse Pali description of existence known as the Three Marks (*tilakkhana*): *anicca dukkha anatta*, which is often translated as "Life is transient, sorrowful, and selfless." In this eidetic formulation about the marks that stain all phenomenon, expanded into verse in the *Dhammapada* (277–279), *anatta* reminds us that the belief in a substantive, enduring self (soul or ego) is an illusion, while *dukkha* emphasizes the First Noble Truth of universal suffering based on selfish desire and clinging to the things of this world (or our thoughts and feelings about those things). Both the latter terms are experientially and logically grounded in the first, *anicca*, which means "not stable, impermanent," and speaks to Shakyamuni Buddha's insight that "whatever is subject to arising must also be subject to ceasing."

With that general statement, the Tathagata is referring to *everything* in our experience—*all* material and immaterial objects, men and women, societies and states of mind, legislation and governments, and to this a physicist would add that even the thirteen-billion-year-old universe itself will one day be reduced to black holes that will eventually disintegrate into stray particles, and these, too, will decay. From the moment of our so-called birth we have been dying, "changing all the time," says Thich Nhat Hanh: "Not a single element remains the same for two consecutive moments."

We can all understand this. There is nothing particularly mystical about the fundamental nature of reality being *change,* process and transformation; nor is there anything esoteric in the wisdom that we err if we desire or try to cling to evanescent phenomena that change faster than we can chase them. In the Buddhadharma, the true nature of things is *sunyata,* or "emptiness." But we would be wrong if we interpreted this emptiness as a *lack* or as vacuous. In his outstanding book *Nonduality,* the scholar David Loy provides a concise account of *sunyata:*

> It comes from the root *śū,* which means "to swell" in two senses: hollow or empty, and also like the womb of a pregnant woman. Both are implied in the Mahāyāna usage: the first denies any fixed self-nature to anything, the second implies that this is also fullness and limitless possibility, for lack of any fixed characteristics allows the infinite diversity of impermanent phenomena.

Those who experience *sunyata* through meditation know that all things from the very first have eternally been in a perfect state of tranquillity, and that

> Suffering alone exists, none who suffers;
> The deed there is, but no doer thereof;
> Nirvana is, but no one seeking it;
> The Path there is, but none who travel it.

In *The Buddhist Vision,* Alex Kennedy (Dharmachari Subhuti) points out that the recognition of impermanence or emptiness necessarily leads to the nonconceptual and discursive intuition that all perceived conditioned and transitory things are interdependent. Thich Nhat Hanh's word for this is "interbeing," a neologism he coined to express the traditional Buddhist understanding of the concatenated links in dependent origination (*pratityasamutpada*). Says Kennedy:

When we analyze any object, we can never come to a substance beyond which our analysis cannot penetrate. We can never find anything conditioned which has an underlying substantial reality. . . . All things, whether subject or object, are processes linked together in an intricate network of mutual conditions. . . . The ordinary man is distracted by the bright surface of the world and mistakes this for reality.

All things are empty in themselves, only existing—as Dr. King said—in a delicate "network of mutuality" where, as we are told in the *Visuddhimagga*, "It is not easy to find a being who has not formerly been your mother . . . your father . . . your brother . . . your sister . . . your son . . . your daughter." After awakening, or the experience of Nirvana, the student of the Way experiences ultimate reality as a We-relation. "Perfect peace," said Shakyamuni, "can dwell only where all vanity has disappeared."

However, in Buddhism, we must acknowledge *two* levels of truth. First, there is ultimate, ontological truth (*paramartha-satya*). In *The Long Discourses of the Buddha*, Maurice Walshe explains that on this level existence is experienced as "a mere process or physical and mental phenomena within which, or beyond which, no real ego-entity nor any abiding substance can be found." Second, there is conventional or relative truth (*samvrti-satya*), described by Walshe as the samsaric world "according to which people and things exist just as they appear to the naïve understanding." (For myself, I enjoy thinking of these two truths in terms of our knowing the subatomic realm of electrons and positrons exists, but in our everyday lives we necessarily conduct ourselves in terms of Newtonian physics because if we step out a tenth-floor window or in front of a fast-moving truck, we will go *splat*.)

The great dialectician Nagarjuna, founder of the Madhyamika school ("Middle Way"), demonstrated that these two truths are not in conflict, because Samsara *is* Nirvana. The sacred *is* the profane. The everyday *is* the holy. The dreamworld of Samsara—of so much suffering—and of relative truth, is the projection of our delusions and selfish desires onto Nirvana. Yet, Samsara is logically prior to and necessary for the awakening *to* Nirvana. The important point here, says John Blofeld in *The Zen Teaching of Huang Po*, is that "the Enlightened man is capable of perceiving both unity and multiplicity without the least contradiction between them." His words echo in the lambent verse of seventeenth-century Buddhist nun Jingnuo, which appears in the wonderful book edited by Beata Grant, *Daughters of Emptiness: Poems of Chinese Buddhist Nuns:* "Everything is in the ordinary affairs of the everyday world." That is, if one is guided by mindfulness, the transcendent is found no less in quotidian tasks such as serving tea, motorcycle maintenance, or the arranging of rock gardens than in the recitation of mantras; no less in washing the dishes, writing this article, or actively participating in mercurial political affairs than in the oldest monastic rituals.

Insofar as Buddhist practitioners grasp reality as a We-relation, they are unshakeable in the experience of the Other as themselves. Thus, in the social and political world of Samsara, there can be but a single proper response to all sentient beings, regardless of their political affiliations or views: compassion and loving-kindness (*metta*). That ethical posture is codified in the bodhisattva vows and in Shantideva's *Guide to the Bodhisattva's Way of Life:*

> First of all I should make an effort
> To meditate upon the equality between self and others:
> I should protect all beings as I do myself
> Because we are all equal in (wanting) pleasure and (not wanting)
> pain.

Hence I should dispel the misery of others
Because it is suffering, just like my own,
And I should benefit others
Because they are sentient beings, just like myself.

When both myself and others
Are similar in that we wish to be happy,
What is so special about me?
Why do I strive for my happiness alone?

For those following the Way individual salvation is never
enough; they work tirelessly for the liberation not just of men
and women but all sentient beings. Politics, therefore, offers the
opportunity to use samsaric means for Nirvanic ends that adapt
the Dharma to those imperfect tools we are obliged to work
with in the relative-phenomenal world. The step on the Eightfold Path called "Right Conduct" demands such conscientious
involvement in the relative-phenomenal realm, for we ourselves
are inseparable from that world and can live, here and now,
nowhere else. But it is *how* the Dharma student works in the
saha-world that is of all importance.

He or she will, I believe, bring one dimension of "Right View"
to the political arena—that is, the understanding that our perspectives and views on a particular issue are not the only veridical
or possible ones. The follower of the Way will practice civility and
"Right Speech," which the *Mahasatipatthana Sutra* says involves
"refraining from lying, refraining from slander, refraining from
harsh speech, refraining from frivolous speech." He or she will
listen with full empathy to the political Other, listening as carefully as they do when following their own breaths and thoughts
in vipassana meditation. They will dispassionately examine evidence, tame their minds, know where their thoughts have come

from, and be able to distinguish what in the mind is the product of past conditioning and received opinion (political ads, propaganda), what thoughts are genuinely their own, and what their desires may be projecting on reality. (We all learned the hard way the importance of this kind of epistemological humility when members of the current administration, driven by their desire for change in the Middle East, rushed into a war with Iraq based on less than reliable "intelligence.") And if peace is their goal, they will in the field of politics be themselves peace embodied. They will work indefatigably in the present moment, but without the beggarly attachment to reward, recognition, or future results; and when disappointment comes, as it must—as it did so often to those unsung heroes of the civil rights movement—Buddhists doing political work would do well not to despair, thinking "*I* have lost, *they* have won," but instead they should remember that no victory won for the Sangha or "beloved community" can last forever (nor any defeat), because every worldly thing is stained by *anicca*. In "defeat," if it comes, they might find solace in a judicious distinction my friend the mystery writer Candace Robb, a Tibetan Buddhist practitioner in Seattle, makes when she says, "Pain is something that comes in life, but suffering is *voluntary* or *optional*" (italics mine). (Or on their refrigerator door they might tape this quote from seventy-five-year-old Master Sheng Yen of the Dharma Drum Cultural Foundation in Taipei: "I follow four dictates: face it, accept it, deal with it, then let it go.") Finally, they will take as a reliable guide for spiritually informed political action the statement Dr. King made in his stirring Nobel Prize acceptance speech exactly forty years ago:

"Civilization and violence are antithetical concepts," he said. "Nonviolence is the answer to the crucial and moral question of our time. . . . The foundation of such a method is love. . . . I have the audacity to believe that peoples everywhere can have three meals a day for their bodies, education and culture for their minds, and dignity, equality and freedom for their spirits."

Dr. King's political objectives in 1964 are, at bottom, of a piece with bodhisattva goals. In our brief passage through this life, we must have both *inner* and *outer* revolutions since the former is essential for deepening the latter. When we no longer divide the great emptiness, *sunyata*, into "this" and "that," we are empowered to reduce without discrimination the suffering of all sentient beings in the *saha*-world. (The term *saha*, as the Buddhist author Robert Thurman informed me, means "almost bearable.")

Naturally *upasakas* and *upasikas* (lay male and female Buddhists) will need the support of their Sangha as they engage in political action. No one understands better the importance of taking refuge in the community of Dharma followers than the Buddhist monk and mendicant Claude AnShin Thomas. Last year he completed the building of a meditation center in Florida as a place where activists can momentarily retire to refresh and renew themselves. This year [2004] his memoir, *At Hell's Gate: A Soldier's Journey from War to Peace,* which in my view is a powerful guide for anyone traveling on the Path of personal and political liberation, will be released in September by Shambhala Publications.

Claude AnShin Thomas understands suffering to be a necessary teacher and "Sangha [as] the entire spectrum of the universe." In his memoir, he reminds us that, as a Buddhist, "I cannot think myself into a new way of living, I have to live myself into a new way of thinking." That wisdom is captured concisely in his reflections on how Dharma followers approach the goal of peace.

"Peace is not an idea," he says. "Peace is not a political movement, not a theory or a dogma. Peace is a way of life: living mindfully in the present moment. . . . It is not a question of politics, but of actions. It is not a matter of improving a political system or even taking care of homeless people alone. These are valuable but will not alone end war and suffering. We must simply stop the endless wars that rage within. . . . Imagine, if everyone stopped the war in themselves—there would be no seeds from which war could grow."

5 | The King We Need:

Teachings for a Nation in Search of Itself

The great problem facing modern man is that the means by which we live have outdistanced the spiritual ends for which we live.
  —Martin Luther King Jr.

WHEN MOST OF US THINK ABOUT that American apostle of nonviolence and peace, Martin Luther King Jr., even some who marched beside him in demonstrations nearly fifty years ago, we do so with an almost deliberate forgetfulness and precious little understanding of the specific "content of character" (to borrow one of King's most famous phrases) displayed by a man who insisted in his sermon "Three Dimensions of a Complete Life" that "somewhere along the way, we must learn that there is nothing greater than to do something for others." Despite the overwhelming presence of this man in our lives, King in his magnificent fullness—as this nation's Socratic "gadfly of the state" and the most prominent moral philosopher in the second half of the twentieth century—is strangely absent. Too many of us, especially those born after his assassination thirty-seven years

ago, see him only in the oversimplified terms of race as an eloquent, segregation-era "voice of his people" frequently and falsely
compared in political conversations with his very different (and
philosophically antithetical) contemporary Malcolm X, whose
daughter's observation in the 1980s about her father's popularity
applies equally as well to King: "He's getting attention, but I
think he's misunderstood . . . Young people are inspired by pieces
of him instead of the entire man."

In other words, these two iconic and long-dead Americans
suffer from the curse of canonization, which progressively over
four decades has airbrushed away the sweat and scars, the pores
and imperfections, and the polyvalence both men exhibited
during their highly influential journeys among us, and this is
tragic, for it is in such personal minutiae that we find the very
foundations from which a memorable public life arises. More-
over, this forgetfulness is a tragedy in 2005 for *all* of us, as Americans, because what is at stake in the Martin Luther King Jr. story
are not only questions about American race relations but also
deeper issues, older conundrums about what it means to be civilized in the political and social world, about how one confronts
social evil without creating evil, division, and enmity, even questions about what Buddhists call *pratitya samutpada* (dependent
origination) that resonate beneath the surface of King's remarkable and too-brief thirty-nine years of life. Clearly, these are
matters of urgency—especially the demand for civility—when
in our spiritually bankrupt world awash in pop-culture vulgarity and terrorist acts (consider the Russian children of Middle
School 1 killed by Chechen rebels and radical Muslim behead-
ings of noncombatants like the Egyptian Mohammed Abdel Aal
in 2004) our leaders during the last presidential campaign, on
both the left and the right, shamelessly employed in their desire
to "win" such tactics as mudslinging and character assassination.

(Prescient, King once stated, "We shall have to create leaders who embody virtues we can respect," and also counseled, "We must be sure that our hands are clean in the struggle.") Would that today's arrogant, thersitical, ankle-biting and so often short-sighted politicians, with their red-meat rhetoric, might remember what King told Freedom Riders in 1960: "Our ultimate end must be the creation of the beloved community."

Sadly, today few if any of King's admirers can list all his campaigns through the South and North, each a drama in itself. (Most only recall Montgomery, Birmingham, and Selma, but what about the battles for equality and justice he led in Albany, Chicago, and St. Augustine, Florida?) Nor can they sketch the complex yet ethically coherent philosophy—part social gospel, part Personalism (the belief that God is infinite and personal), and part Gandhian *satyagraha*—that led him triumphantly from the Montgomery bus boycott in 1955 to the Nobel Peace Prize in 1964, and produced that breathtaking fusion of scholarship and idealism known as "Letter from Birmingham Jail," one of the great political documents in American history, which King composed in a darkened cell without a single note or textbook to refer to, writing first on the margins of a newspaper, then on toilet paper, and finally on a legal pad provided by his lawyers.

Fewer still know anything about the role religion played in his family's lineage (his father, Daddy King, was a prominent Atlanta minister and activist, of course, but his grandfather Adam Daniel Williams was known to preach the "funerals of snakes, cats, dogs, horses, or anything that moved"); or his childhood and parents ("It is quite easy for me to think of the universe as basically friendly," King wrote in 1950, "mainly because of my uplifting hereditary and environmental circumstances"); or his education that culminated in a PhD from Boston University when he was twenty-five (he began his freshmen year at Morehouse College when he was fifteen years old, and was a disciplined, star student at Crozer Theological Seminary); or his personal regimens, eccentricities, spiritual goals; or even the name of one of his favorite sermons—the one he believed captured the essence of his message—among all the speeches he gave during his fourteen-year public ministry.

It was not, as so many believe, the impromptu speech King delivered on August 28, 1963, during the March on Washington when he tossed aside the words he'd worked on until 4:00 A.M. that day, but rather "The Drum Major Instinct"; his lifelong friend Rev. Ralph Abernathy played a recording of that powerful sermon at King's funeral. Taking his text from Mark 10:35, where James and John, the sons of Zebedee, approach Jesus with their desire to sit beside him in Glory, King said:

> There is, deep down within all of us, an instinct. It's a kind of drum major instinct—a desire to be out front, a desire to lead the parade, a desire to be first. And it is something that runs a whole gamut of life. . . . We all want to be important, to surpass others, to achieve distinction, to lead the parade. Alfred Adler, the great psychoanalyst, contends that this is the dominant impulse . . . this desire for attention. . . . Now in adult life, we still have it, and we really never get by it. We like to do something good. And you know, we like to be praised for it. . . . But there comes a time when the drum major instinct can become destructive. And that's where I want to move now. . . . Do you know that a lot of the race problem grows out of the drum major instinct? A need that some people have to feel superior. Nations are caught up with the drum major instinct. I must be first. I must be supreme. Our nation must rule the world. . . . But let me rush on to my conclusion. . . . Don't give it up. Keep feeling the need for being important. Keep feeling the need for being first. But I want you

to be first in love. I want you to be first in moral excellence. I want you to be first in generosity. That's what I want you to do."

If moral authority is based on moral consistency, then the above statement, which King felt encapsulated his life's palmary work and vision, demonstrates why this liberal theologian became a leader admired by all Americans and world citizens of goodwill, for he lived his own advice in "The Drum Major Instinct," from his childhood when Daddy King counseled Martin, who was born into the class of black Atlanta Brahmins, against feelings of class superiority to the final days of his life when he was preparing the Poor People's Campaign for economic justice. If I read King's life correctly, there are three discernible stages in the public evolution of this man who was both the creator and creation of one of the most transformative moments in American history. His early, pre-Montgomery years are, of course, fascinating in their own right; in her biography, *My Life with Martin Luther King Jr.,* Coretta Scott King speaks of how

> if he ever did something a little wrong, or committed a selfish act, his conscience fairly devoured him. He would, throughout his life, really suffer if he felt there was some possibility that he had wronged anyone or acted thoughtlessly. He was a truly humble man and never felt he was adequate to his positions. This is why he worried so much, worked so hard, studied constantly, long after he became a world figure.

Coretta was, we should note, a graduate of Antioch College, and says she "took to my heart the words of Horace Mann, who founded Antioch. In his address to the first graduating class he had said, 'Be ashamed to die until you have won some victory for humanity.'"

Her husband, Martin, believed as she did, and he says as much in "Three Dimensions of a Complete Life." There, in one of his favorite sermons—the first he preached at Dexter Avenue Baptist Church in Montgomery—King described life's essentials in terms of length, breadth, and height. The first, length, concerns the development of the individual. "After we've discovered what God called us to do, after we've discovered our life's work, we should set out to do that work so well that the living, the dead, or the unborn couldn't do it better." The second dimension, breadth, highlights our social relations: "Don't forget in doing something for others that you have what you have because of others. . . . We are tied together in life and in the world." And finally, said King, at the center of the last dimension, height, is our relationship to the divine. "We were made for God, and we will be restless until we find rest in him."

So, yes, he was by temperament and training prepared at age twenty-five to have thrust upon him the leadership of the Montgomery bus boycott when Rosa Parks refused to give up her seat to a white man on December 1, 1955. In this first stage of his public life, the exquisitely learned, young scholar who had not yet experienced the traditional, numinous moment of religious conversion (his awakening would come later in his kitchen during the height of threats against his family) became the American symbol for the struggle against segregation, and the ideals of integration and brotherhood wore *his* face. But why him? Why not other respected activists like, say, Congressman Adam Clayton Powell or the NAACP's Roy Wilkins? The answer to that question can be found on the night of January 30, 1956, when King, who was at a meeting, learned his home had been bombed. He rushed there, found Coretta and their baby, Yolanda, unharmed, and outside an angry, armed black crowd spoiling for a showdown with white policemen at the scene. The situation was edging toward violence. King raised one hand to quiet the crowd, and then said, "I want you to go home and put down your weapons. We cannot solve this problem through retaliatory violence. We must meet violence with nonviolence. . . . We must meet hate with love." Later, the policemen would say King saved their lives. His Gandhi-esque stance, his agapic vision, was heard round the world as something uniquely redemptive in the bloody, centuries-long struggle for black liberation in America.

King's calming words, in the heat of racial violence, were an American's skillful adaptation of Gandhi's observation that "hatred does not cease by hatred at any time. Hatred ceases by love. This is an unalterable law." ("Christ furnished the spirit," said King, "Gandhi showed me how it worked.") That was the law of King's life and political vision in the 1950s and early 1960s. "Power at its best," he said, "is love implementing the demands of justice; justice at its best, is love correcting everything that stands against love." Championing such wisdom resulted in his receiving fifty assassination threats, the wrath of J. Edgar Hoover's FBI, and the envy (and sometimes opposition) of Black Power activists. A $30,000 bounty would be placed on his head. He would be stabbed once (in Harlem by a mad black woman named Izola Curry), arrested and jailed again and again. Despite all that, King embraced as a Christian much of what a Buddhist would see as the bodhisattva vows; he traveled to India in 1959, a guest of the Gandhi Peace Foundation, and returned to America determined to devote one day a week of his ever strangulation-tight schedule to fasting and meditation.

In this initial phase of King's public life, his core beliefs can be expressed, as I argue in my novel *Dreamer* (1998), in three transcendentally profound theses. First, that nonviolence—in words and actions—must be understood not merely as a strategy for protest but as a Way, a daily praxis men must strive to translate into each and every one of their deeds, so that, in its fullness King's moral stance implies noninjury (*ahimsa*) to everything that exists. Consider, please, how this translates into the ten points of the "Commitment Blank," a kind of Decalogue signed by members of the Southern Christian Leadership Conference (SCLC) and their followers during the electrifying Birmingham campaign:

COMMANDMENTS FOR THE VOLUNTEERS

I HEREBY PLEDGE MYSELF—MY PERSON AND BODY—TO THE NONVIOLENT MOVEMENT. THEREFORE I WILL KEEP THE FOLLOWING COMMANDMENTS:

1. *Meditate* daily on the teachings and life of Jesus.
2. *Remember* always that the nonviolent movement seeks justice and reconciliation—not victory.
3. *Walk* and *talk* in the manner of love, for God is love.
4. *Pray* daily to be used by God in order that all men might be free.
5. *Sacrifice* personal wishes in order that all men might be free.
6. *Observe* with both friend and foe the ordinary rules of courtesy.
7. *Seek* to perform regular service for others and for the world.
8. *Refrain* from the violence of fist, tongue, or heart.
9. *Strive* to be in good spiritual and bodily health.
10. *Follow* the directions of the movement and of the captain on a demonstration.

(When SCLC's activists operated on the basis of these vows, they could not fail in winning the hearts and minds of their opponents, for clearly they approached their "enemy" as themselves.)

Secondly, he urged us to practice *agape,* the ability to uncon-
ditionally love something not for what it presently is (for at a
particular moment it might be quite unlovable, like the segrega-
tionist George Wallace in the early 1960s) but instead for what
it could become, a teleological love that recognizes everything as
process, not product, and sees beneath the surface to a thing's
potential for positive change—the kind of love every mother has
for her (at times) wayward child.

And last, he understood integration and interdependence to
be the life's blood of our being, proclaiming, "It really boils down
to this: that all life is interrelated. We are all caught in an inescapable network of mutuality, tied in a single garment of destiny.
Whatever affects one directly, affects all indirectly." In effect, King
understood that our lives are *already* tissued, ontologically, with
the presence of Others in a We-relation the recognition of which
moves us to feel a profound indebtedness to our fellow men and
women, predecessors and ancestors. "When we get up in the
morning," he said, "we go into the bathroom where we reach for
a sponge provided for us by a Pacific Islander. The towel is provided by a Turk. We reach for soap created by a Frenchman. In the
kitchen, you drink coffee provided by a South American, or tea by
a Chinese, or cocoa by a West African, and you butter toast from
an English-speaking farmer. And before you've finished breakfast,
you've depended on more than half the world. . . . This is the way
our universe is structured. This is its interrelated quality. We aren't
going to have peace on earth until we recognize this basic fact of
the interrelated structure of the universe." And if our destinies are
so intertwined, it follows that "strangely enough, I can never be
what I ought to be until you are what you ought to be. You can
never be what you ought to be until I am what I ought to be."

Little wonder, then, that when King entered Stage Two of his
evolution, which I date from the day he received the Nobel Peace

Prize, he envisioned himself not merely as a southern civil rights leader but instead as a man obligated to promote his belief in the "beloved community" and peace on the world stage—a stance that would make him the first international celebrity to oppose the Vietnam War (and a comrade of a young monk named Thich Nhat Hanh, whom King nominated for that prize). In 1964, at age thirty-four, he was the youngest person to receive the peace prize. The money came to $54,000, and King kept none of it for himself. He divided the prize money evenly between five organizations devoted to civil rights and peace. Forty-one years ago, in his acceptance speech for the award, he told his audience: "Civilization and violence are antithetical concepts. Nonviolence is the answer to the crucial and moral question of our time. . . . The foundation of such a method is love. . . . I have the audacity to believe that peoples everywhere can have three meals a day for their bodies, education and culture for their minds, and dignity, equality, and freedom for their spirits."

But it was inevitable that King, after seeing so many victories for humanity—from Montgomery to the passing of the Civil Rights Act in 1964 and Voting Rights Act in 1965—would question what he should do next. Those closest to him said he experienced bouts of depression. His critics wanted to see him retire permanently to his church in Atlanta, or take a quiet job as president of a black college. He said to his friend Bayard Rustin, "I sometimes wonder where I can go from here. I've accomplished so much. What can I do now?" It was this question after 1965—what *now*—that propelled King into Stage Three of his development, returning him to a conclusion he noted about our economic life as early as 1951: "It is a well-known fact that no social institution can survive when it has outlived its usefulness. This capitalism has done. It has failed to meet the needs of the masses."

This last and greatest "dream" called for reforming capitalism to end poverty once and for all, an issue still of concern for voters during the 2004 presidential election. For King, that goal translated, specifically, into an Economic Bill of Rights, the redistribution of wealth, and a guaranteed income for all Americans. The superb historian Stephen B. Oates wrote eloquently of this final phase in *Let the Trumpet Sound: The Life of Martin Luther King Jr.*:

> This hardly made King a Marxist. He meant it when he told his staff that Marx "got messed up" when he failed to "see the spiritual undergirding of reality" and embraced an odious "ethical relativism" which led him to believe that the ends justified the means. And King continued to preach against the evils of Russia's dictatorial communist state. No, somehow a better social order than communism or capitalism had to be constructed, one that creatively blended the need for community and the need for individuality. Perhaps in this, his most imaginative, desperate, and far-reaching scheme, he could take his country a step closer to the realization of an old dream: the forging of a Christian commonwealth.

In hindsight, we know that King's promotion of what I would call Christian Socialism influenced a generation of black American leaders, from Huey Newton of the Black Panthers to Rev. Jesse Jackson. Had he lived and realized his "Washington Project" of leading the poor of all races and ethnic backgrounds to shut down the nation's capital, King might have become the most dangerous man in America—the one public figure, much revered, who could potentially unify in his person and through the power of his moral authority the civil rights, labor, and antiwar movements.

But that was not to be. A metal-jacketed 30.06 bullet ended his life on the balcony of the Lorraine Motel in Memphis on April 4, 1968, and with his death a glorious, tempestuous chapter in the history of this republic ended. That same year in one of his last sermons, "Unfulfilled Dreams," King said, "And I guess one of the great agonies of life is that we are constantly trying to finish that which is unfinishable." He understood, as must we all, that hard-won spiritual and political triumphs can be lost in a single generation. In her biography, Coretta also speaks about the problem of achieving a final victory for the ideals of social and economic justice in a world of change and impermanence.

"One of the failings of the Movement," she wrote, "was that, while we taught people to fight against the system, and how to respect themselves, we didn't teach young people that they would have to fight all over again. As long as we have a democratic system we are going to have to work to protect our freedom and self-respect. And that is for blacks or whites or whatever color. Freedom is never guaranteed forever; you have to fight for it."

6 | Why Buddhists Should Vote

FOR A FREE PEOPLE THE FRANCHISE means everything. In a democratic republic, it is the proper name for empowerment. It is the essence of political equality. As Rev. Joseph Carter put it in St. Francisville, Louisiana, in 1963, "A man is not a first-class citizen, a number-one citizen, unless he is a voter."

But for nonwhite Americans and women, exercising this constitutional right involved a long, painful struggle from the nation's founding to the passage of the Voting Rights Act of 1965. This legislation, one of the primary goals of the civil rights movement, was achieved only after the agony of numerous campaigns sponsored by the National Association for the Advancement of Colored People, the Congress of Racial Equality, Student Nonviolent Coordinating Committee, and the Southern Christian Leadership Conference to register eligible black voters throughout the South. There, blacks who tried to vote were savagely beaten. Or hanged. They faced economic reprisals. Their homes were burned, their families driven out of town. Whites dropped snakes on those who stood in line to register. They obstructed black voters with preposterous "literacy tests" (when many illiterate whites were registered) and state poll taxes that were not outlawed in federal elections until the passage of the Twenty-Fourth Amendment in 1964. In a word, American blacks paid for the precious franchise with their lives, among them the civil rights worker James Chaney, who along with the white "Freedom Summer" volunteers Michael Schwerner and Andrew Goodman was murdered for trying to register blacks in Mississippi.

I've recited this grim recent history because, as a Buddhist, I've long viewed the sphere of politics—and especially racial politics—to be the perfect illustration of Samsara, or what the two-thousand-year-old sutra *The Perfection of Wisdom* calls *kamadhatu*: "the realm of desire" characterized by dualism and the hunger for power. It is a highly competitive world of Them vs. Us. Of "winners" and "losers," where the Buddhist insight into "impermanence" is given concrete form as laws that may last only as long as the time between two elections. As one history teacher informed me when I was an undergraduate, one useful way to interpret any political document or piece of legislation is by first identifying in it the "screwer" and the "screwee," who always seem present in political affairs. No Buddhist I've known has ever been interested in playing either one of those parts.

But for all my aversion to the polarizing dimensions of politics, I cannot forget the legal scholar Edward S. Corwin's observation that the Constitution is "an invitation to struggle," which in the context of Dharma means struggle in the politicized realm of Samsara—and doing so with the ironic understanding that, from an absolute standpoint, no one is struggling at all. And what does a Buddhist struggle *for* in the realm of relativity? The answer, I think, is twofold: to alleviate the suffering of all sentient beings and turn the wheel of Dharma.

One way to read the injunction for "Right Conduct," which is an essential part of the Eightfold Path, is to see it as calling us—as citizens—to translate the Dharma into specific acts of social responsibility. In a democratic republic that surely means voting for those initiatives that we believe will reduce suffering and violence, ignorance, and hatred—and the very divisions fueled by politics itself. (Since the word for "right" in Sanskrit, *samyak*, is the same as for "perfect," I prefer to call this "Perfect Conduct," because that avoids the dualism inherent in the word "right," which inevitably conjures up its opposite "wrong.")

Thus, a Buddhist would not hesitate to vote for legislation and political candidates devoted to peace, to undoing injustice, reducing *dukkha* in its myriad manifestations, healing society's wounds, preserving individual freedoms, and protecting the environment as well as the rapidly vanishing forms of plant and animal life that are a part of it (and what Nhat Hanh calls our "interbeing"). I do not feel that a Buddhist—whatever his or her tradition or lineage—must necessarily join a political party, for that often entails a blind allegiance that puts the party's survival and "winning" elections ahead of the ethical behavior outlined in the "Eightfold Path." Rather, one can remain an "independent," supporting life-nurturing proposals and propositions wherever they arise, among Democrats or Republicans, the left or the right. (Once again, the Samsaric language of a two-party political system plunges us into dualism!)

And yet, having just presented my arguments for why Buddhists should vote, I'm reminded of Dr. King's warning that only the spiritual life can lead to his goal of the "beloved community." "Racial justice . . . ," he wrote, "will come neither by our frail and often misguided efforts nor by God imposing his will on wayward men, but when enough people open their lives to God to allow him to pour his triumphant, divine energy into their souls." In Buddhist terms, we *must* vote and use the means of the relative-phenomenal world to reduce suffering, for we are part of the relative-phenomenal world. But suffering *will* continue, despite our best efforts, until all of us experience—like Shakyamuni Buddha—enlightenment and liberation.

7 | Is Mine Bigger than Yours?

EVERY DAY I LURK AND LISTEN TO the scholars of Eastern religions on Buddha-L (the Buddhist Academic Discussion Forum), taking notes when their exchanges clarify some arcane matter of Pali grammar or touch upon sutras I feel I should study. This academic forum is moderated by the scholar Richard Hayes, and on June 28, 2007, he insightfully examined the meaning and implications of the Sanskrit word *maana*.

"According to some abhidharma traditions," wrote Dr. Hayes,

one of the last obstacles that a person overcomes on the road to liberation is *maana*, usually translated as pride. . . . In abhidharma literature, *maana* is described as the tendency to think in one of three ways: (1) Thinking of oneself as better than others; (2) Thinking of oneself as inferior to others; and (3) Thinking of oneself as equal to others. . . . The Sanskrit word is derived from a verbal root that means to measure. So *maana* is the act of measuring, or perhaps comparing. It is the kind of thinking we do when we wonder, whether to ourselves or out loud, "Is mine bigger than yours? Is mine as good as yours?" Abhidharma is right, I think, in pointing out that all of us who are not arhants (and

I'm guessing that would be several of us on Buddha-l) are busy measuring ourselves against the standards set by others.

Then Dr. Hayes adds,

> Having acknowledged that we are all prone to looking around to see how well we stack up in comparison to others (for we are, after all, social animals, and we learn best by imitation) and whether we're still okay in the imagined eyes of other beholders, even those we pretend to disregard, I think one can cultivate the habit of focusing so much on flaws that one fails to see what is good in things.

Every dimension of our lives—personal and professional, even our miscellaneous list of "likes" and "dislikes"—is saturated with *maana*. From our earliest years of receiving grades that measure our academic progress to the promotions we strive for on our jobs, *maana* is an activity we engage in every minute of every day.

If we did not do this measuring in the realm of conventional reality (or *samvrti-satya*), we would be unable to function socially or practice "Right Effort" when we see our discipline becoming lax. But *maana* can be spiritually damaging to others and ourselves (I'm thinking now of one of the Dalai Lama's interviews when he was asked, "How shall we deal with self-hatred?," and H.H. found the question so confounding—almost an oxymoron for a Buddhist who knows an enduring "self" is an illusion—that he asked the interviewer for an explanation for what in the world "*self*-hatred" could possibly mean); and it is at odds with the precepts that we "do not speak of others' errors and faults" and "do not elevate self and blame others."

Fortunately, in the *Mahasatipatthana Sutra*, the Buddha offers an antidote for *maana* that I have always found to be infallible: namely, "contemplating mind as mind . . . mind-objects as mind-objects." The mind, being the exotic phenomenon that it is, churns out 24/7 thoughts and feelings that are wholesome and unwholesome, kind and unkind. We have to sit patiently with this extraordinarily colorful mind (and ourselves). All manner of thoughts and memories arise ("I feel sad," "That hurts," or "That was nice," "I'm great," or "I'm a loser" or as we read in the *Dhammapada*, "He abused me; he beat me; he defeated me; he robbed me"). We do not judge these thoughts and feelings. Or ourselves for having them. We don't embrace or run from them. We simply let them *be*, observing how like all impermanent things they are ephemeral, transitory, like bubbles in a stream, rising and fading away. A feeling of anger at someone might arise, but we know that *we* are not this anger. If we do not grasp at or cling to it, its energy will dissipate. And as we inspect each mind-object, we are free, of course, to pursue those that are wholesome, kind, and enable us to alleviate the suffering of others, allowing those thoughts to become actions.

The result of this practice is an opening of one's heart to others, to ourselves. It also leads to "epistemological humility," which is a healthy skepticism about what we think we know. For example, this spring my wife and I will celebrate our fortieth wedding anniversary. I have known her since we were twenty years old. I have seen her change over more than four decades. I know her as a friend, mother, confidante, spiritual seeker, former teacher, and social worker. I know her medical history and the results of her DNA testing. I know her human birth to be a blessing unknown to either gods or hungry ghosts. But I can never know all her thoughts, feelings, and experiences even after a lifetime spent together. Do we ever truly "know" another well enough to judge them as better, equal, or inferior to ourselves when each of us is, ontologically, a ceaseless play of patterns—physically, emotionally, perceptually, and in respect to consciousness? I think not. To some degree, the Other remains a wonderful mystery that ever outstrips our concepts, feelings, and perceptions of her. My wife, therefore, is always new and surprising to me. We can say the same about ourselves. And in the face of such mystery, as we contemplate ourselves and others, the Buddhist approach is to do so with egoless listening to how the Other presents herself, phenomenologically, to us moment by moment. Another name for such selfless listening is love.

This, I believe, is what is meant in the statement attributed to Shakyamuni Buddha (perhaps apocryphal but certainly in the spirit of Dharma) that "you yourself, as much as anybody in the entire universe, deserve your love and affection."

8 | Why Buddhism for Black America Now?

What I propose is a spiritual revolution.

  —His Holiness the Dalai Lama

IN HIS 1970 WORK, *Buddhist Ethics*, Hammalawa Saddhatissa writes in the preface, "Strictly speaking, Buddhism is not a religion in the generally accepted sense of the word, and it would be more accurate to describe it as an ethico-philosophy to be practiced by each follower. And it is only by practice, by an uphill spiritual struggle, that happiness in life either present or future, as well as the goal of *Nibbāna*, can possibly be attained." For this conference, I was asked to discuss some of the implications of this ethical philosophy for black America, and also ways it might relate to the civil rights movement. These issues are matters that I've spent a lifetime thinking about, but for me this is not merely an academic discussion. Rather, I see it as a matter of life and death for black Americans. Let me try to explain what I mean by that.

Like the narrator of Charles Dickens's novel *A Tale of Two Cities*, many black Americans today possibly feel "It was the best of times, it was the worst of times." The reason is because, as Eugene Robinson explained in an April 4, 2008, article in the *Washington Post*, there are actually two very culturally different black Americas as this new millennium begins.

In one profile, black Americans appear in every walk of life and profession. They are millionaires, even billionaires, having earned their wealth in business, sports, and entertainment. (Beyonce Knowles last December gave her husband, Jay-Z, whose fortune is worth $450 million, the most expensive car in the world, a Bugatti Veyron Grand Sport priced at $2 million; a month later Oprah Winfrey premiered her own network, appropriately named OWN; and Kanye West just spent $180,000 for a watch in his own image, which is only slightly less than the $250,000 that rapper Usher paid a New York luxury watch company to create a timepiece with *his* face on it.) But in a different, grim, and depressing portrait, 25 percent of black Americans live in poverty. That percentage in 2011 may become even higher after what we call the Great Recession, which pushed members of the fragile black middle class into the ranks of the poor. Seventy-one percent of black babies are born out of wedlock and over half of black children (56 percent) are fatherless. In America's prisons, where on average the 2.25 million persons incarcerated in 2006 had fewer than eleven years of schooling, about half are black. One in nine black men between the ages of twenty and thirty-four is in prison. While black people represented 13 percent of the US population in 2005, they were the victims of 49 percent of all murders, 15 percent of rapes, assaults, and other violent crimes nationwide, and most of the black murder victims—93 percent—were killed by other black people. In 2008, the black male high school graduation rate in Baltimore, Maryland, dropped to 25 percent, was 50 percent in Chicago, and in California ten thousand black students (42 percent) quit school. And to these dire figures we must add the fact that nearly six hundred thousand blacks have the AIDS virus, with their rate of death two and a half times that of whites who have been infected.

A report published last November [2009] by the Council of the Great City Schools, entitled "A Call for Change," states that "the nation's young black males are in a state of crisis" and describes their condition as "a national catastrophe." This report shows that

> black boys on average fall behind from their earliest years. Black mothers have a higher infant mortality rate and black children are twice as likely as whites to live in a home where no parent has a job. In high school, African-American boys drop out at nearly twice the rate of white boys, and their SAT scores are on average 104 points lower. In college, black men represented just 5 percent of students in 2008.

Commenting on this situation, Ronald Ferguson, director of the Achievement Gap Initiative at Harvard, said, "There's accumulating evidence that there are racial differences in what kids experience before the first day of kindergarten. They have to do with a lot of sociological and historical forces. In order to address those, we have to be able to have conversations that people are unwilling to have."

The "sociological and historical forces" Ferguson refers to were also identified as the origin of this contemporary problem a few years ago by Adjoa Aiyetoro, then director of the National Conference of Black Lawyers, who said, "One of the issues we deal with every day is the vestiges of our enslavement, and our post-enslavement in this country has been such that it has beat us down as a people in so many ways." If there was an essence or *eidos* for black life during slavery and the seventy years of racial segregation that followed it, that invariant meaning would have to be *craving*, and the quest for identity and liberty.

Legal segregation ended a little less than fifty years ago, within living memory for some of us. And today, the syndicated columnist Bob Herbert, writing about the dismal education report published in November, described this current situation in the post–civil rights period as a "raging fire that is consuming the life prospects of so many young blacks." "Cultural change comes hard," he said, "and takes a long time, but nothing short of profound cultural change is essential." This feeling that a new way of thinking is necessary was expressed even earlier by one of the icons of the civil rights movement, John Lewis. "If King could speak to us today," Congressman Lewis said in 1994,

> he would say, in addition to doing something about guns, he would say there needs to be a revolution of values, a revolution of ideas in the black community. He would say we need to accept nonviolence not simply as a technique or as a means to bring about social justice, but we need to make it a way of life, *a way of living.*

So this is an old problem, one I've witnessed my entire life; and, like John Lewis, I'm old enough to remember Dr. Martin Luther King's concern with the interplay between the personal and the political. "We must work on two fronts," he said. "On the one hand we must continually resist the system of segregation—the system which is the basic cause of our lagging standards; on the other hand, we must work constructively to improve the lagging standards which are the effects of segregation. There must be a rhythm of alteration between attacking the cause and healing the effects." And in his sermon "Rediscovering Lost Values," delivered on February 28, 1954, at Detroit's Second Baptist Church, King railed against "relativistic ethics," "pragmatism" applied to questions of right and wrong, and the "prevailing attitude in our culture," which he described as "survival of the slickest." King knew that we have a "culture" for young black males that catches them up in gangs, despair, fatherlessness, drugs, prison, anti-intellectualism, and antisocial behavior by the time they are eight years old. We have created obstacles, traps, and racial minefields for young black men, and long demonized them as violent, criminal, stupid, lazy, and irresponsible. This conversation that "people are unwilling to have" is obviously one that we must begin if we want young, black American males to no longer be "an endangered species," as some people have described them, and if we want them to survive in the highly competitive, global, knowledge-driven economies of the twenty-first century. I'm convinced that in terms of what we traditionally call "ethics," the twenty-six-hundred-year-old Dharma of Buddhism must be part of that conversation.

In 2003, *Turning Wheel,* the journal of socially engaged Buddhism, devoted a special issue to "Black Dharma." In that issue, Rebecca Walker, the daughter of the writer Alice Walker and a well-known Buddhist writer herself, interviewed the Vajrayana teacher Choyin Rangdröl. Last year, Rebecca informed me that she and Lama Rangdröl, whom she met at the first black American Buddhist retreat in 2002 at Spirit Rock in Woodacre, California, are now married. During that interview, she asked him, "What led to your decision to bring the Dharma to African Americans?" He replied, "When I discovered that it was possible to avoid becoming ensnared in the mentality of an angry black man by applying Buddhism, I felt I had found a great treasure not just for me but also for resonance in millions of black people's minds."

Equally interesting is a 2003 interview in *Tricycle* with George Mumford, a sports psychologist who teaches vipassana meditation to the Chicago Bulls and Los Angeles Lakers, and who overcame years of drug and alcohol addiction. "I came to Buddhist practice because I had *dukkha, dukkha, dukkha*," said Mumford. "Excuse my language, but my ass was on fire. My life depended on meditation practice. . . . I got into Twelve Step recovery and lo and behold, I had pain, I had to deal with a lot of chronic pain—migraines, headaches, back aches. And emotional pain and spiritual pain." Mumford then discovered vipassana, the practice taught worldwide with such success by Satya Narayan Goenke. Mumford reports, "I learned that I could control my mind. No matter what happened to me, I could choose my response to it. I had lived in fantasy all my life. Once I started getting involved in meditation, I realized that I did have an alternative. It was the first time I had a sense of control in my life."

"I think the main benefit of meditation for inner-city African Americans," he added,

> is impulse control. The inner city is a pressure cooker, full of tension and anxiety. It's easy to go off or to reach for something to ease the pain. Meditation helps people understand the operation of their minds and emotions. It teaches us how to detach ourselves from outside provocation and from our habitual patterns of reaction. Now, I'm not suggesting that we should take abuse and racism and all that other stuff, and just breathe in, breath out. That's something else. But the first thing we have to do is have control of ourselves, and then we can choose with a clear mind.

Just in passing, I think it's important to say that Mumford states that all his uncles were alcoholics and died at a young age. His father was an alcoholic, too, and violent toward his family. Mumford confesses, "I knew the taste of beer before I could walk. At fifteen or sixteen, I started snorting heroin." The dilemma he faced is one that is not uncommon for all the at-risk young black men I mentioned at the start of this talk, the ones who succumb in adolescence (or preadolescence) to the group pressure of gangs, substance abuse, and criminal behavior. But Mumford discovered vipassana, a tool for analyzing and rebuilding his world at its source: the mind. This is one of the beauties of the Buddhadharma. Instead of simply proclaiming what we should do, it shows us how to extend compassion from ourselves to even our so-called enemies through spiritual techniques and algorithms—for example, the five steps of the *metta* meditation. I believe young black males (and females) should begin the practice of meditation at the earliest age. In 2010, researchers at the University of Cambridge took 155 boys from two schools in the United Kingdom, and put them on a crash course in mindfulness training. After the trial period, the fourteen- and fifteen-year-old boys were "found to have increased well-being, defined as the combination of feeling good (including positive emotions such as happiness, contentment, interest and affection) and functioning well." The researcher behind this project, Professor Felicia Huppert, said, "We believe that the effects of mindfulness training can enhance well-being in a number of ways . . . calming the mind and observing experiences with curiosity and acceptance not only reduces stress but helps with attention control and emotion regulation—skills which are valuable both inside and outside the classroom."

Vipassana has also proven to be effective at the William G. Donaldson Correction Facility, an overcrowded prison in Alabama. There, one third of the fifteen hundred inmates convicted of murder, sex offenses, and robbery are on death row or serving sentences of life without parole. The inmates at this facility were the subject of a 2007 documentary called *The Dhamma Brothers*, and what they have done has become a model for other prisons. In 2002, forty inmates met four times a year in the prison gym for an intense ten-day course in mindfulness training. Dr. Ronald Cavanaugh, the prison's treatment director, reported that after this experience, "the inmates are less angry, better able to conduct themselves, they're more mindful of themselves and others, and overall there has been a 20% reduction of disciplinary action for those who have completed the course."

The historical and present-day suffering experienced by black Americans creates a natural doorway into the Dharma. Dr. Jan Willis has been identified as the first black American scholar-practitioner of Tibetan Buddhism. She is an esteemed scholar of religion and East Asian studies at Wesleyan, where she has taught for thirty years, and is the author of a moving memoir entitled *Dreaming Me: From Baptist to Buddhist, One Woman's Spiritual Journey.* In 2009, she received the Outstanding Woman in Buddhism award for her work on behalf of Buddhist nuns, specifically her cofounding in 1995 a nunnery that houses fifty Buddhist nuns ages forty-two to eighty-three in India. "People of color," said Willis in an interview, "because of our experience of the great and wrenching historical dramas of slavery, colonization, and segregation, understand suffering in a way that our white brothers and sisters do not." That understanding, she said, provides a kind of "head start" in comprehending essential elements in Buddhist philosophy.

For Dr. Willis, like Thich Nhat Hanh, Buddhism and Christianity, the religion historically associated with black Americans, are not in conflict. "I can use *Buddhist* methods," she said, "to practice *Baptist* ideals." This sidestepping of an apparent conflict based on dualistic thinking is made possible because the Dharma—or teachings—is wisdom not monopolized by the cultures of the Far East. For a Buddhist, this approach of "both/

and" as opposed to "either/or" is made possible by the condition of dependent origination, *pratitya samutpada*, which describes all conditioned phenomena as arising from a concatenation of causes, and this makes all phenomena interdependent and interconnected. Thich Nhat Hanh, who has an image of Jesus in his place of meditation, refers to this ontology as "interbeing." So aspects of the Dharma are as easily discovered in Western and black American culture as they are in Eastern ones, in Christianity as well as Islam, because the Buddhist experience *is* the human experience. If one looks closely one can see some of its elements in the *Meditations* of Marcus Aurelius; in the Rhineland sermons of Meister Eckhart; in Hume's critique of the self in *A Treatise of Human Nature*; in George Washington's advice on how best to select one's friends (which echoes the advice offered in the *Rhinoceros Sutra*); and in the aphorisms the writer Jean Toomer published in his book *Essentials* and in his 1937 poem "Blue Meridian." In other words, we only call ourselves "Buddhists" for the sake of convenience in a world attached to labels. Some practitioners simply say they are "students of the Dharma." Others do not identify or label themselves at all.

Jan Willis, Lama Rangdröl, Mumford, Walker, the Zen teacher Angel Kyodo Williams, and the approximately fifteen thousand black practitioners of Soka Gakkai (Nichiren) Buddhism, who chant chapters of the *Lotus Sutra,* belong to the first black generation in America to recognize the relevance of the Dharma for the specific historical and existential forms of suffering that are the residue of slavery and racial segregation in a very Eurocentric country; and they believe this practice may satisfy John Lewis's call for "a revolution of values . . . of ideas in the black community," a revolution that encourages nonviolence as "a way of life." Like their black predecessors, the law of their lives—their historical inheritance—is the quest for liberation. They wish to be free. *Truly* free. This first-wave, new generation of black American Buddhists includes in its ranks politicians like Georgia Congressman Hank Johnson, a member of Soka Gakkai International; entertainers such as Tina Turner; and the jazz great Herbie Hancock, who in a 2007 interview for Beliefnet said,

> The idea of cause and effect, which is what *Nam-myoho-renge-kyo* is about, made sense to me. I'm a guy that's always been at-tracted to science—and cause and effect is what science is about. . . . The cool thing is that jazz is really a wonderful example of the great characteristics of Buddhism and the great characteristics of the human spirit. Because in jazz we share, we listen to each other, we respect each other, we are creating in the moment. At our best we're nonjudgmental. If we let judgment get in the way of improvising, it always screws us up. So we take whatever happens and try to make it work. . . . At the same time—and just think about this—within the life of a human being is the universe. So, we all have the universe inside at our core.

Clearly, Mr. Hancock does not have an image of himself based on his being in any way "inferior" or a "victim." Those conceptualizations can poison the mind and the human spirit. He is not mired in a past that cannot be recovered or a future that will never come, but instead works to anchor himself "in the moment." Like Lama Rangdröl, he is not ensnared in the debilitating, bitter, polarizing, clichéd "mentality of an angry black man." And Hancock's comparison of his egoless listening and nonjudgmental approach as a jazz musician to the Dharma reminds us that Buddhist practice has much in common with the process we associate with creating art, which demands openness to all phenomena.

The black American practitioners I've presented, all representing different branches (or traditions) of the bodhi tree, have seen in Buddhist practice the most revolutionary and civilized of possible human choices, one that extends King's dream of the "beloved community," especially in terms of the Dharma's emphasis on addressing the "second front" Dr. King told us we must not neglect. One thing that is essential for this spiritual revolution is *ahimsa*, doing no harm to other sentient beings and ourselves. You need only to pick up today's newspaper to see that the world in which we live, and our enveloping culture, is saturated through and through with violence, all manner and degrees of violence in our dualistic ways of thinking, our actions, our speech, and even in our forms of popular entertainment. And this has been so for a very long time. I mentioned slavery and segregation, two social arrangements that could only be maintained through systematic, institutional violence. But I could also mention the political violence in our time, from the assassinations of King, Malcolm X, both Kennedys, and so many others in the 1960s to the recent shooting of Rep. Gabrielle Giffords and killing of six others, including a nine-year-old girl, in Arizona. Historically, we *are* a violent nation. And it is violence and anger more than anything else that we must "let go." But we need clear, practical guidelines to do that.

In the Buddhist world, the Ten Precepts are commonly found among many traditions. They are taken by laity and monks alike, and I took them in the Soto Zen school with the mendicant monk and peace activist Claude AnShin Thomas. The first ten vows are as follows:

1. Do not kill.
2. Do not steal.
3. Do not engage in improper sexual conduct.

4. Do not lie.

5. Do not indulge in intoxicating substances.

6. Do not speak of others' errors and faults.

7. Do not elevate self and blame others.

8. Do not be withholding, but instead generous.

9. Do not give way to anger.

10. Do not defame the Buddha, the Dharma, or the Sangha.

Whenever I describe these precepts to friends in the academic and art worlds, many of them balk and say, "I can't *do* that" when they hear number 5 ("Do not indulge in intoxicating substances"), numbers 6 and 7 ("Do not speak of others' errors and faults," and "Do not elevate self and blame others"), and especially number 9 ("Do not give way to anger"). In their honesty, they admit that being nonjudgmental, as Hancock said of his practice, is extremely difficult in our society—a society that so often portrays the angry person as a powerful person, and finding fault as a proper intellectual activity that demonstrates our critical acumen, shows our intellectual superiority and, by virtue of that, feeds our egos. In this culture, then, it is difficult to let go of pride (*maana*), and anger, which is a form of violence and one of the three defilements, along with greed and ignorance, though Saddhatissa points out in *Buddhist Ethics*, "By allowing anger to arise I am like one who wants to hit another and picks up a burning ember or excrement and by so doing either burn or soil myself." Although simple and straightforward (and, of course, demanding), the precepts embody the spirit of the Four Noble Truths, the Eightfold Path, the *paramitas*, and in them we can see the distillation of Buddhist metaphysics.

The faintest experience of Nirvana or *sunyata*—the emptiness at the heart of all things—extinguishes like a candle's flame the craving and thirst (*trishna*) described in the First and Second

Noble Truths. For Mumford, who said his "ass was on fire," this extinction of craving allowed him to tame Vivekananda's conditioned and erratic "monkey mind," and to understand through mindfulness the operations of his own consciousness—how we perpetually see through the veil of our ideas or Samsara, which Mumford called "fantasy." Black American Buddhists understand that the reality we experience is our creation, and how we respond to it is our personal responsibility. They are as politically sophisticated, aware of the history of oppression, and concerned with social justice as their predecessors. But they have located a "middle way" between withdrawal from social life, on the one hand, and surrendering to the egoistic pursuit of things cheap, banal, and self-centered, the vulgar hedonism and desire for ephemeral baubles promoted 24/7 by capitalism and America's adolescent youth culture. As Geshe Wangyal might put it, they live in "detachment without denial; involvement without indulgence."

In order to appreciate why the theologian Paul Tillich once called Buddhism "one of the greatest, strangest, and at the same time most competitive of the religions proper," and why it is attractive to black Americans in the post–civil rights era, we must see that Buddhism neither accepts nor rejects the idea of God. Why? First, because one's happiness and salvation, awakening and liberation from suffering, rests entirely in one's own hands (i.e., the karmic cause and effect relationship that so impressed Herbie Hancock). Second, the understanding of *anicca*, or impermanence, contained in the Buddha's observation that "whatever is subject to arising must also be subject to ceasing," is the ontological starting point for Buddhist reflection on all things. This begins with the experience of emptiness or the lack of an enduring, separate, immutable, and unchanging essence or substance in everything. That realization, which was systematically expounded by the Buddhist philosopher Nagarjuna, leads naturally to the perception of dependent origination. In this vision, the "self" we struggle so hard and long to bolster and sustain is discovered to be a construct at best. Static (racial) identity is an illusion. We are constant change, reborn moment by moment. We have no nature, no essence, no self, no substance as our identity—and no relation whatsoever to the evil, racist iconography that caricatures black people in popular culture and the national consciousness. It is *that* kind of essentialism that gives rise to attractions and revulsions, our attachments and clinging, and to prejudices that lead to *dukkha*. In his article "No Religion," Buddhadasa Bhik-khu presents a provocative interpretation of the meaning of birth, death, and being reborn. "For example," he says,

> think like a criminal and one is instantly born as a criminal. A few moments later those thoughts disappear, one thinks like a normal human being again and is born as a human being. If a few moments later one has foolish thoughts, right then one is born as a fool. . . . Thus, in a single day one can be born any number of times in many different forms, since a birth takes place each and every time there arises any form of attachment to the idea of being something. Each conception of "I am," "I was," or "I will" is simultaneously a birth.

Something also attractive to black American practitioners is the fact that in its proto-empiricism and with its flavor of phe-nomenology, early Buddhism rejects any reliance on *apta vacana* (received opinion) or appeals to an authority. As the Buddha says in the *Kaulama Sutra,*

> Do not go by oral tradition, by lineage of teaching, by hearsay, by a collection of scriptures, by logical reasoning, by inferential

reasoning, by reflection on reason, by the acceptance of a view after pondering it, by the seeming competence of a speaker, or because you think, "The ascetic is our teacher." But when you know for yourselves, "These things are unwholesome, these things are blamable; these things are censured by the wise; these things, if undertaken and practiced, lead to harm and suffering," then you should abandon them.

The Buddha also taught:

Look within!
You are the Light itself.
Rely on yourself.
Do not rely on others.
The Dharma is the Light.
Rely on the Dharma.
Do not rely on anything,
Other than the Dharma.

We can take the first small steps toward this inward revolution called for by the Dalai Lama, and the cultural revolution in black communities called for by Congressman Lewis, by mindfully changing the way we talk to each other—precepts numbers 6 and 7—by eliminating the unwholesome violence and disrespect in our speech. I would like to suggest a simple test for whatever you want to say *before* you say it. Think of this test as being three questions—or three doors—your speech must pass through before you make it public. The first door is, *Is it true?* The second door is, *Is it necessary?* And the third door is, *Will it cause no harm?*

The goal of the Buddhadharma is to extinguish the war within, and to help Americans black and white realize complete liberation—even from the concepts of the Dharma, if they cause us to be attached or to cling to that which is impermanent and unsatisfactory. More radical than any other "religion," it also makes clear that when Buddhist ideas such as the Four Noble Truth, the Eightfold Path, the practices and *paramitas* have served their purpose, these are ethical guidelines that we will eventually "let go," like the proverbial raft that carries us safely across the sea of Samsara, for once we reach the other shore, it is no longer necessary to carry even that vehicle on land. Ironically, and like no other religion or philosophy, the Dharma enables us to free ourselves even from itself.

9 | Mindfulness and the Beloved Community

IF WE WISH TO UNDERSTAND THE special meaning that the Buddhadharma has for blacks in America—and why in the twenty-first century it may be the next step in our spiritual evolution toward what Martin Luther King Jr. called the "beloved community"—we need look no further than the teaching of mindfulness, which is the root and fruit of all Buddhist practice. In Sanskrit, the word for mindfulness is *smriti*, which means "remembrance, recollection or memory." One important variation on *smriti* is *smritimat,* which means "possessing full consciousness." Bhikkhu Bodhi explains this core Dharma teaching succinctly when he says:

> The task of Right Mindfulness is to clear up the cognitive field. Mindfulness brings to light experience in its pure immediacy. It reveals the object as it is before it has been plastered over with conceptual paint, overlaid with interpretations. To practice mindfulness is thus a matter not so much of doing but of undoing: not thinking, not judging, not associating, not planning, not imagining, not wishing.

For black Americans in the post–civil rights period, this systematic *undoing* of the cultural indoctrination, the "conceptual paint" we have received from a very decadent, violent, materialistic, and Eurocentric society, is crucial for our liberation, personally and as a people. The situation of being a racial minority in a predominantly white country—this provincial, Western fishbowl, or "wasteland," as T. S. Eliot described it—is rife with ironies and dangers. One of the greatest ironies is that black Americans for centuries *had* to be open to more than one cultural orientation. We had to know how to "read" American society in at least two ways—first, in terms of what we knew about the enormous contributions African Americans have made to this country since the seventeenth-century colonies, a knowledge gleaned from other black people, and from unrecorded stories transmitted by family members and friends, which whites ignored, didn't know, or marginalized in their history books and "mainstream" media. Second, we had to understand, as any social (or racial) outsider must, the cultural formations of a WASP society simply because such intimate knowing of the white Other was necessary for navigating successfully through America's institutions (schools, jobs, social situations, etc.).

That "double consciousness," as W. E. B. Du Bois put it one hundred years ago in *The Souls of Black Folk,* creates a valuable critical distance. When you look at American materialism and decadence, Du Bois said in 1926, "you know in your heart that these are not the things you really want. You realize this sooner than the average white American because, pushed aside as we have been in America, there has come to us not only a certain distaste for the tawdry and flamboyant but a vision of what the world could be if it were really a beautiful world."

We know that until recently the white *Weltanschauung* was myopic and blissfully ignored the history, lives, and philosophical visions of people of color, privileging and prioritizing instead the ideas, texts, and experiences of whites as the universal standard for the good, the true, and the beautiful. This is, of course, to be expected in a country where those of European descent still control so much of the cultural apparatus that shapes public (and popular) consciousness. If one is in the majority, *un*enlightened, and holds the reins of power in the realm of Samsara—the world of racial dualism, egotism and Them vs. Us—one naturally defines the world in one's own (white) image.

There is much of great value in the Western world, but many WASPs too often are, sadly, hesitant to experience the world beyond the parochial fishbowl they have created. This is a form of spiritual and intellectual laziness we black people *cannot* afford if we hope to survive in a society long hostile to us. From the beginning of our Western experience we have been positioned, culturally, to be *open* to *all* racial Others, to explore and absorb multiple visions of human experience, Western and Eastern. We are a people forged, as the writer Albert Murray once said, as "Omni-Americans."

That openness to, say, the East can serve us well in contemporary America. For in today's Western fishbowl, the American mind, black or white, is conditioned day and night to resemble the famous "monkey mind" described by the nineteenth-century philosopher Vivekananda in *Raja Yoga:*

> There was a monkey, restless by its own nature, as all monkeys are. As if that were not enough, someone made him drink freely of wine, so that the monkey became still more restless. Then a scorpion stung him. When a man is stung by a scorpion, he jumps about for a whole day; so the poor monkey found his condition worse than ever. To complete his misery a demon entered into him. What language can describe the uncontrollable

restlessness of that monkey? The human mind is like that monkey, incessantly active by its own nature; then it becomes drunk with the wine of desire, thus increasing its turbulence. After desire takes possession comes the sting of the scorpion of jealousy of the success of others, and last of all the demon of pride enters the mind, making it think itself of all importance. How hard to control such a mind.

How difficult, indeed, especially for black people who know America is still, for the most part, a racially balkanized nation, and who find here so many negative images of themselves mirrored back by popular culture. Fortunately, the Buddhadharma provides, through mindfulness and other meditational practices, time-honored techniques for taming the labile mind. For undoing the received and generally biased interpretations of the world (and Madison Avenue's endless propaganda of having and getting) with which this society bombards all its citizens. Those practices deliver to us, phenomenologically, a perception of the world *before* it has been mediated by the language of samsaric influences, for mindfulness is, if nothing else, the practice of radical attention. Of clear seeing. Of listening, which is one of the attributes of *metta* (loving-kindness). When we practice moment-by-moment mindfulness, or vipassana ("insight meditation"), we carefully and dispassionately observe all that arises and passes through the mind, but without clinging or attachment. After decades of practice, we trust, as Shakyamuni Buddha counseled his followers, only what is empirically *given* in our direct experience, and we let go the illusions created by social conditioning, by a flawed, Eurocentric educational system, and by a language steeped in metaphysical dualism. The result, as Alex Kennedy reminds us in *The Buddhist Vision,* is that the practitioner of Dharma tames his mind, knows where his thoughts have come from, is able to distinguish what in the mind is the product of past conditioning and what is genuine. He lives in the *here* and *now*. He is epistemologically humble, respecting the mystery that lies at the heart of Being. And he knows as well that whatever we find of value in our life's experiences—all the teachers and texts and practices—are simply *tools* to serve our enlightenment and liberation. After we have crossed to the "other shore," we can "let go" these tools, just as one would not cling or be attached to a boat after it has taken us across the sea (of suffering).

Among the unnecessary baggage that mindfulness allows us to "let go" is the tragic belief in a separate, enduring (black) self. It slashes away, as effectively as does Ockham's razor (which says we should avoid postulating entities to account for what can be explained without them or, scientifically, when presented with two hypotheses that explain something, it's best to select the simpler one), the narrow, obscuring ego. When that ego is gone we experience a long-deferred peace. In fact, we will *be* peace embodied. We will experience not only solace in the face of life's general sufferings (sickness, old age, and death) but also a clarifying refuge from white racism, and certain crippling, samsaric aspects of black American life, by which I mean the socially conditioned *thirst* and attachment too many black people have for transitory, material possessions and ephemeral pleasures that have been so long denied. Reams have already been written about the devastating effects that black-on-black crime, drugs, gang violence, the high incarceration rate for young black men, and the preponderance of single-parent homes have on our now-fragile communities. These dysteleological aspects of black life do not simply have sociological and economic causes. Behind those we find deeper layers of selfish desire, much self-inflicted suffering, and the chimera of the ego.

Such problems can only be addressed if the Revolution first begins *within* each and every one of us. Only if we can let our hearts flower open 24/7 to a life of nonviolence (physically and verbally) and to *ahimsa* ("harmlessness") toward all sentient beings who, after all, want only the same two things we do—happiness and to avoid suffering. And only if we tame our tempestuous "monkey minds" through the daily practice of mindfulness, which can be realized anywhere and at any time: when we sit, walk, wash the dishes, or do *any* worldly task, for in Buddhism there is no distinction (or dualism) between the sacred and profane.

As the great dialectician Nagarjuna revealed to us, Samsara *is* Nirvana. The everyday *is* the holy. The dreamworld of Samsara— of so much suffering—is the projection of our and others' sedimented delusions and selfish desires (Bhikkhu Bodhi's "conceptual paint") onto Nirvana. Yet, when those delusions and desires are extinguished, we—as a people—will know greater joy, freedom, and abundant creativity; and we will realize, like the poet Bunan, the transcendent beauty and liberation that lies beyond a false sense of dualism:

The moon's the same old moon,
The flowers exactly as they were,
Yet I've become the thingness
Of all the things I see.

10 | The Meaning of Barack Obama

THERE ARE MANY THINGS WE CAN say about the historically unprecedented campaign of Senator Barack Obama to become America's first nonwhite president, but one thing we can certainly expect the general election in November to do is take the temperature of racial attitudes in America at the dawn of a new century. For Buddhists, awakening is the goal of our practice. After decades of meditation, daily spiritual practice, and study of the Dharma, we find ourselves acutely aware of how intellectual constructs can create illusion or ignorance (*avidya*) and fuel divisiveness and dualism in our lives. Clearly, one of the most toxic of these illusions is the notion of "race." To be sure, it is a political issue. But more importantly, it is an enlightenment issue as well.

By now we know—or *should* know—that race is our grandest lived delusion and grief-causing fiction: "a social construction," says the Stanford University historian Richard White, who in a *Seattle Times* article in 2001 reminded us that at one time the Irish, Jews, Poles, and southern Europeans were excluded from the exclusive social club of "whiteness." As scientists continue sequencing the genome, they find no biological basis for race. Sharon Begley's 2003 "Science Journal" column in the *Wall Street*

Journal reported, "Geneticists find that when they add up the tiny genetic variations that make one person different from the next, there are more differences within races than between races."

"Race has no basic biological reality," Jonathan Marks, a Yale University biologist, reported in a Knight-Ridder newspaper article. "The human species simply doesn't come packaged that way." Other scientists in that same 1996 article agreed with Marks, among them the Stanford geneticist Luigi Cavalli-Sforza, who said, "The characteristics that we see with the naked eye that help us distinguish individuals from different continents are, in reality, skin-deep. Whenever we look under the veneer we find that the differences that seem so conspicuous to us are really trivial."

Yet, for all that, we continue to live the lie of race, which according to an article in a 2003 issue of *Science News* (November 22) literally makes us stupider. "White people who hold biased feelings toward blacks have to work to control their thoughts and behaviors during interracial encounters," says the psychologist Jennifer Richeson of Dartmouth College in Hanover, New Hampshire, and her coworkers. "This social strategy depletes the limited pool of mental resources available for monitoring and using various types of information."

Even before the current popular interest in DNA research, Guy Murchie wrote brilliantly in his book *The Seven Mysteries of Life* (1978) that if we trace our ancestry back fifty generations to 700 C.E., we find we all share a common ancestor. None of us, Murchie insists, can be less closely related than fiftieth cousins. "Your own ancestors," he wrote,

> whoever you are, include not only some blacks, some Chinese and some Arabs, but all the blacks, Chinese, Arabs, Malays, Latins, Eskimos and every other possible ancestor who lived on earth around to A.D. 700. . . . It is virtually certain therefore

that you are a direct descendent of Muhammad and every fertile predecessor of his, including . . . Confucius, Abraham, Buddha, Caesar, Ishmael and Judas Iscariot.

My point, if it isn't clear yet, is that race is *maya*. A chimera constructed for reasons of social, political, and economic domination, and for the comfort of fragile, insecure egos.

Furthermore, it is difficult not to recognize that interpenetration of backgrounds that transcend dualism in the biography of Barack Obama. There is the white mother from that most iconic of states in pop culture (Kansas, for heaven's sake, Toto), the Muslim father from Kenya (which makes Obama genuinely *African* American), his formative years spent in Indonesia and his Indonesian half-sister, and Hawaii (a state of considerable multicultural diversity). Indeed, his clearly multiracial background, like that of Tiger Woods or Halle Berry (and, if we scratch ourselves deeply enough, all of us), is an indication of a demographic that will only vividly increase in the twenty-first century, with the generic and misleading terms "white" and "black" consigned to the dustbin of human history. (Of the 1.76 million people who filled out the 2000 Census, one in twelve black Americans under age eighteen checked multiple boxes to indicate their identities.)

So one must be willfully blind to have missed this cosmopolitan, globe-spanning background and sensitivity in Obama's speeches. In fact, it is primarily this seldom explicitly stated subtext, and not his particular policy positions, that made the initial public response to Obama after the Iowa primary nothing short of *primal*, and he and Michelle the stuff that dreams are made of, symbols for a new century and its desire to transcend tribalism and the barriers between people. Crowds have even cheered when Obama blew his nose. With little political history or baggage to weigh him down (which for his opponents is his Achilles' heel), Obama is, as he himself said, a kind of blank slate onto which Americans have projected their deepest and most visceral social and cultural longings. For black people, the promise of his becoming president was the "impossible dream" their ancestors had nurtured since the era of slavery; for whites, a president of color—especially one who in his speeches transcends several decades of balkanization along the lines of race, class, and gender—meant that the ideals of equality and opportunity enshrined in the nation's most sacred documents, the Declaration of Independence and the Constitution, were not just fine-sounding words but instead a tangible possibility that might take place in our lifetime. And across the planet, from Africa (one newspaper headline in Kenya called him "Our Super Power Son") to the Middle East (in a Muslim nation, a proverbial man on the street told reporters the freshman senator looked like people he saw every day), Obama's seemingly exotic but in fact common background was inspirational because, as he said to an audience of two hundred thousand in Germany during his ten-day visit to other nations, he is an American who views himself as "a fellow citizen of the world."

At a time when the prestige of the United States has been badly damaged by the invasion of Iraq, and so many of its allies feel alienated from the Bush administration, Obama's sincere interest in dialogue and diplomacy suggest that bridges between the world's last superpower and other nations—especially in the developing world—might be repaired. The only thing Obama has rejected outright is extremism, as represented by his former pastor Rev. Jeremiah Wright and by Rev. Michael Pfleger.

Neither Eurocentric nor Afrocentric as a leader, Obama seems at "home" in Africa and the East; leading a University of Chicago Law School seminar or organizing for the poor on that city's South Side; or on the reservation of the Crow Nation, where he was adopted under the name "One Who Helps People throughout the Land." There, he acquired the alias "Barack Black Eagle." Obama seems to wear those names as easily as he did the yarmulke he wore during his visit to Jerusalem's two thousand-year-old Western Wall, where he slipped between the beige stones a handwritten prayer, which should have remained private (someone gave it to the newspaper *Maariv*), but once published it provided us with a brief glimpse into his soul: "Lord—Protect my family and me. Forgive me my sins, and help me guard against pride and despair. Give me the wisdom to do what is right and just. And make me an instrument of your will."

Predictably, Obama's universality has triggered both confusion and criticism. In one of his August columns, David Brooks said,

> There is a sense that because of his unique background and temperament, Obama lives apart. He put one foot in the institutions he rose through on his journey but never fully engaged. . . . This ability to stand apart accounts for his fantastic powers of observation, and his skills as a writer and thinker. It means that people on almost all sides of an issue can see parts of themselves reflected in Obama's eyes. But it does make him hard to place. . . . If Obama is fully a member of any club— and perhaps he isn't—it is the club of smart post-boomer meritocrats. . . . They are conscientious and idealistic while also being coldly clever and self-aware. It's not clear what the rest of America makes of them.

What Mark Penn, Hillary Clinton's top campaign strategist, made of this was a possible attack strategy in his March 2007 memo—wisely never used—based on his feeling that Obama did not have "roots to basic American values and culture." Perhaps

Brooks and Penn did not understand that one characteristic of men and women who follow a spiritual path is that they often appear to "be not conformed to this world" (Romans 12:2). Rather, they are fully engaged serving others yet detached (*viragyam*) at the same time.

Eloquent and elegant, charismatic and holding a degree from Harvard Law (where he served as the law review's president), relatively young compared to establishment politicians, always comfortable in his skin, tall and lean in a Lincoln-esque way, Obama (as well as his wife, Michelle) is also an avatar of a new black America in the post–civil rights period: namely, two generations of high-achieving, disciplined black professionals—historically *transitional* generations—whose achievements are everywhere evident in fields as diverse as business, the sciences, education, law, and the entertainment industry. Has the hour arrived, then, for a member of this generation to move into the White House?

Perhaps it would be best to describe the Obama phenomenon as being, from a Buddhist perspective, not so much revolutionary as it is potentially *evolutionary*. But if that is so, then one problem Obama faces are people who do not want to evolve beyond the ancient stupidity and error of epidermalizing the world, who cling or are attached to the idea of a racial (or geographic) identity as a way of avoiding the experience of their true nature as interconnectedness or emptiness (*sunyata*). Or, if you prefer existentialist thought to the Buddhadharma, see this in terms of Sartre's famous statement, "Existence precedes essence." In other words, the meaning of our lives is never pre-given; whatever meaning we find is based on our deeds, actions, and, as Martin Luther King Jr. once said, "the content of our character." The senator from Illinois, who repeatedly in his statements rejects obsolete ways of thinking and talking about race, predictably finds himself walking a cultural tightrope, always performing with balance, remarkable grace, and civility when attacked by those with a tribal mentality (white, black, and otherwise) who feel most threatened by the monumental sea change his presence in American politics represents. If his campaign fails, it may well be for the reason Charles M. Blow identified in an August 9 op-ed in the *New York Times*: the inability of the monkey mind in a majority of American voters to "let go" the illusion of race. If he wins, we may have the possibility of a bit of liberation and relief from centuries of racial masks and dissembling.

For Obama understands that a black presidential hopeful can only become the leader of the most powerful nation in human history if he rises above the racially provincial and parochial—and if his humanity, empathy, and compassion are strongly felt to be genuine by his "fellow citizens of the world." That is one enduring lesson of this dramatic, unprecedented campaign. And whether he wins or not in November, the truth that excellence is color-blind, and that broad service to others has no tribal affiliation, will live on in our memories long after the general election is over.

11 | Every Twenty-Eight Hours:
The Case of Trayvon Martin

OVER THE LAST WEEK WE'VE HEARD a great deal about how a Florida jury reached a verdict of not guilty for George Zimmerman in the death of Trayvon Martin. We've seen an international response of outrage over this decision. But something we've seen little of is a serious discussion of the daily, centuries-old demonization of black men that festers like a disease beneath Martin's death. Perhaps for supporters of Zimmerman, Trayvon did or did not act wrongly on the day he was killed, but he had to be guilty of *some*thing—some previous crime or sin or moral slippage. For to be a black male in white America means to be wrong, to be less. His essence is that of a predator. The meaning of his life is "thug," someone about whom Zimmerman could say when he called 911, "This guy looks like he's up to no good or he's on drugs or something. . . . These assholes, they always get away."

As a sixty-five-year-old black male, and now the grandfather of a sixteen-month-old grandson, I know this problem intimately because I've been on its receiving end all my life. On my twentieth birthday in a suburb of Chicago, I was quite surprised that I had survived that long. Both my son and I have been forced to unwillingly perform in the universal ritual for black males when, like Trayvon Martin, we were stopped by the police in New York and Seattle for simply "walking while being black." All we have to do to be reminded of our racial wrongness in a Eurocentric society is step outside our door, where the possibility of being ambushed by a new racial wound (or death) awaits us, where someone or something will let us know our presence is unwelcome.

This negative socialization of black boys begins as early as elementary school. In his recent book, *Pursuing Trayvon Martin: Historical Contexts and Contemporary Manifestations of Racial Dynamics*, the philosopher George Yancy observes, "As black, I am possessed by an essence that always precedes me. I am always 'known' in advance. Please welcome the 'person' who needs no introduction: *the black . . .*" He reminds us that "the first American edition of the *Encyclopedia Britannica* (1798) described 'Negroes' as being cruel, impudent, revengeful, treacherous, nasty, idle, dishonest, and given to stealing." Or as the antiracism activist Tim Wise puts it, "Black males are, for far too many in America, a racial Rorschach test, onto which we instantaneously graft our perceptions and assumptions, virtually none of them good."

Beneath the legal and political nightmare of the Zimmerman verdict is a deeper cultural, moral, and spiritual nightmare, one that for a Buddhist or anyone else is all about ignorance (*avidya*) and a long-postponed awakening for white America. "It's not the Negro problem, it's the white problem," James Baldwin famously said many decades ago. "I'm only black because you think you're white."

Because of this willful blindness to the complexity of black men, we have now lost *two* generations of our young people.

Martin belongs to a *third*. In a recent article by Robin D. G. Kelley, he states that, "According to data compiled by the Malcolm X Grassroots Movement, a black person is killed by the state or by state-sanctioned violence every twenty-eight hours." Something I can't help but notice in stories about the death of black males in that "endangered" range between the ages of fourteen and thirty-four is how little their deaths seem to matter. Even if they hadn't gone to jail or been killed, no one assumes they'd be anything more than a low-skill or unskilled worker at best. No one speaks (as Buddhists do) of the importance of their achieving a human birth, or sees them as being unique individuals with promise, talents, resources, or even genius that one day might improve this republic. The underlying, unstated assumption confronting every black boy from a very early age is that they are not going to do anything important or valuable (except perhaps in entertainment or sports, which are another form of entertainment). They are never going to become, say, president of the United States, or a great artist, scientist, spiritual leader, or make any sort of significant contribution to the lives of others. Does anyone other than Trayvon's parents or Rachel Jeantel have any idea what he hoped to one day be? (His father says he dreamed of being a pilot.) Do we ever wonder if black men dream? Do we honestly believe they are more than victims or predators, and that their dreams, intellects, and the daring of their imaginative pursuits *could* enrich society if they were given the kind of support and encouragement historically reserved for white boys and girls?

We rightly feel anger over all the Trayvons murdered billions of times every day by toxic perceptions and conceptions in the white mind, and then, tragically, murdered every twenty-eight hours for real. Six years ago, in the Ten Precepts that I embraced in the Soto Zen tradition, I vowed to not nurture anger. But every feeling or thought that enters consciousness, even anger, can strengthen the practice of a mindfulness that might extinguish at its root this endless cycle of early death for young black men. Bhikkhu Bodhi once explained mindfulness this way:

> The task of Right Mindfulness is to clear up the cognitive field. Mindfulness brings to light experience in its pure immediacy. It reveals the object as it is before it has been plastered over with conceptual paint, overlaid with interpretations. To practice mindfulness is thus a matter not so much of doing but of un-doing: not thinking, not judging, not associating, not planning, not imagining, not wishing.

For white America, this systematic *undoing* of centuries of racial indoctrination, this letting go of the "conceptual paint" it has uncritically absorbed about black Americans, is the necessary first step toward the epistemological humility and egoless listening we are morally obliged to bring to our encounters with all Others. Another name for such selfless, healing listening is love.

PART TWO

Reviews and Prefaces

12 | A Full-Bodied Zen

THAT PERENNIAL GEM OF CH'AN Buddhism, *Zen Flesh, Zen Bones: A Collection of Zen and Pre-Zen Writings*, published in 1957 by Paul Reps, came into my life in 1969 when I was a twenty-one-year-old undergraduate philosophy major at a Midwestern university, a young black American cartoonist and martial artist who first practiced meditation at age fourteen and devoured every Buddhist, Taoist, and Hindu work in translation that I could get my hands on.

What utterly transformed my way of seeing in *Zen Flesh, Zen Bones* was its final, two-page section, simply titled "What Is Zen?" Twice that question is asked on its penultimate page. Two traditional answers are given, extending to the bottom of (unnumbered) page 175, with the last line being "Another answer." Completely engrossed by the question, I turned the page of my Doubleday Anchor edition, eager to experience the final answer, my intentionality focused like the beam of a flashlight, only to discover the last page was blank, an expanse of emptiness into which my mind unexpectedly plummeted. This was no accident. It was wickedly skillful means. The text's very design and format literally forced me to "empty my cup," plunging my desire for "another answer" suddenly into a tantalizing glimpse of satori; and after a timeless moment of silence—my mind cleared of its usual mental panorama, both question and questioner, subject and object momentarily gone—I laughed out loud with joy and a frisson of liberation on the rocking, rattling Illinois Central train I was riding between Carbondale and Chicago during school break. But these numberless pages were only a fraction of the beauty to be found in *Zen Flesh, Zen Bones*. The book consists of four judiciously chosen documents, the first three originally compiled by Reps in the 1930s, and these represent his collaboration on the transcription with the Buddhist scholar and wandering monk Nyogen Senzaki.

In part 1, "101 Zen Stories," we are treated to Dharma tales from the thirteenth-century *Shaseki-shu* ("Collection of Stone and Sand") written by the Japanese Zen teacher Muju, and to them Reps adds numerous anecdotes of Zen monks published in Japanese texts early in the twentieth century. Here, readers will find classic stories reprinted so often in the West since the 1950s that we experience them again as we would dear, old friends—"A Cup of Tea," "Muddy Road," and "The Moon Cannot Be Stolen," brief and brilliant narratives that remind us how "Zen spirit has come to mean not only peace and understanding, but devotion to art and to work, the rich unfoldment of contentment, opening the door to insight, the expression of innate beauty, the intangible charm of incompleteness."

Part 2, "The Gateless Gate," offers forty-nine famous koans recorded by the Chinese master Ekai (Mu-mon) in his thirteenth-century *Mu-mon-kan* ("no gate barrier"), with Mu-mon's commentary included. Once again, the form here is that of a story— each a Dharma drama—about Zen teachers and their students whose "word-drunkenness and mind-wandering" the koans correct. Among the best-known are "Gutei's Finger," "Joshua Washes the Bowl," and "Nansen Cuts the Cat in Two," but all are treasures a practitioner will want to return to again and again. Their aim, wrote Reps, is to eliminate "the dualistic, outgoing, generalizing, intellectualizing tendencies of students in order that they might realize their true nature." It is impossible to call any one of the book's sections my favorite, but part 3, "Ten Bulls" (also known as the "Ten Oxherding Pictures"), has always been a series of spiritual drawings that I've cherished, so much so that they inspired my second novel, *Oxherding Tale* (1982), a comic slave narrative about a nineteenth-century bondsman's quest for manumission and *moksha*. The version we find in *Zen Flesh, Zen Bones* is identical to the transcendent ten pictures of the twelfth-century artist Kakuan Shien, which depict the spiritual stages that lead to enlightenment by portraying the search of a young herdsman for his lost ox (self); but here the simple and elegant illustrations are provided by the Kyoto woodblock artist Tomikichiro Tokuriki. One can study them for days or decades, as indeed I have because I downloaded Tokuriki's drawings as a screensaver for my PC. "Centering," the book's fourth gift, is Reps's bringing together of aphorisms and meditation instruction from four-thousand-year-old Sanskrit texts and traditions (Vigyan Bhairava, Sochandra Tantra, and Malini Vijaya Tantra) that predate Zen and remind this reader of the Buddhadharma's prefiguration in India's diverse wisdom teachings—the Vedas and Advaita Vedanta, for example—as well as Western literature for, as Reps writes, "Zen is not a sect but an experience."

Rich in spiritual and cultural artifacts that are our global inheritance as human beings, *Zen Flesh, Zen Bones* belongs, I truly believe, in every Dharma practitioner's library.

13 | Going Beyond Ethnic Dualism

IN COUNTLESS STORIES THAT RECORD an American's odyssey
to Buddhism we repeatedly find the broad outline of a spiritual
paradigm: first, there is the experience of *dukkha* or suffering in
one (or more) of its myriad samsaric manifestations, followed
by exposure to the teachings of the Tathagata, and finally the
embracing of a practice that leads to enlightenment and liberation. However, for black Americans suffering takes a uniquely
pernicious and psychologically damaging racial form—namely,
the seismic blows to self-esteem in a society where blacks have
since the seventeenth century been defined as this country's "Un-
touchables." Yet seldom, if ever, do we acknowledge in our apolit-
ical and nonracial discussions of Buddhism the fact that for many
black Americans the "three jewels" of the Buddha, the Dharma,
and the Sangha provide, like Christianity, not only solace in the
face of life's general sufferings (sickness, old age, and death) but
also a clarifying refuge from white racism, Eurocentrism, Western
hegemony, and even certain crippling aspects of black American
culture itself during the tender, beginning stages of one's practice.

It is timely, then, that as a new millennium begins and
Buddhism enters its twenty-sixth century, two black American

women have published books that attempt to provide insights into how the Dharma can undo the damage inflicted on the embattled psyches of people of color.

The first of these works is *Dreaming Me: An African American Woman's Spiritual Journey* by Jan Willis, who describes herself as a "Baptist-Buddhist." Even if Willis, a Sanskritist and Indo-Tibetan scholar at Wesleyan University, had never heard of Buddhism, her inspiring memoir would nevertheless be the narrative of a fascinating American life. Raised near Birmingham, Alabama, in Docena, a former mining camp frequently terrorized by Ku Klux Klan cross-burnings, Willis went to segregated schools and saw up close the brutality unleashed upon civil rights activists in 1963. For example, she and her family marched during the Birmingham campaign and were only a few feet away when Sheriff "Bull" Connor's dogs tore at the trousers of a black man, an image captured in what is now one of the movement's classic and most frightening photographs. The world of Willis's youth was one in which "many black children had been blinded by acid or hot lye thrown through open car windows." A fear-drenched world where, she writes, all the signs and signals around her "told us that we were less than human, a people cursed by God to live degraded lives; told us that we were lazy, stupid, and unfit for society."

Despite these oppressive childhood experiences, Willis's intellectual ability (she skipped one grade and fell only two points shy of attaining Mensa status on an IQ exam) won her a scholarship to Cornell, which she entered in 1965 as one of only eight African-American students. There, she majored in philosophy, spent her junior year studying Buddhism in India, and as a senior transported guns to members of the Black Student Alliance that took over Cornell's student union in 1969. Increasingly torn between her attraction to Buddhism and the violent militancy of the

Black Panther Party, which she almost joined, between "a piece or peace," as she puts it, Willis opted for returning on a fellowship to a Tibetan Buddhist monastery in Nepal, where the year before she had been warmly welcomed by the head monk who told her, "You should stay here and study with us."

During her period of study at the Gelukpa Monastery, Willis met lama Thubten Yeshe, who lived nearby in Kopan and became her beloved teacher for fifteen years. "I had come to Lama Yeshe loaded down with guilt, shame, anger, and a feeling of utter helplessness," she writes. "I couldn't think or see past the rage I felt from the untold indignities I'd experienced in life prior to meeting him. Such anger had crippled me in countless ways and had almost sent me down the path of violence. Yet, wounds like mine had a flip side, too, a false and prideful view of entitlement: Look at all that I've endured. I'm great."

Her practice, that of Tantric Buddhism, with its emphasis on "deity-yoga" (visualizing oneself as infinitely compassionate, wise, and fearless) combined with "voidness-yoga," meditation and mantra, enabled Willis to begin the arduous, decades-long task of dissolving the many negative conceptions of herself accumulated since childhood. To let go of her rigid clinging to the self. To see her hatreds for what they were. ("Emotions," a Tibetan friend tells her, "are empty. They come from the mind; but they come and go.") Practice brought her to a place where she was able to "sit right down in the middle of [her] problems and wounds, welcome them in, and look at them squarely and directly with focused yet relaxed concentration." And, finally, it let her achieve for several days a "tantalizingly blissful awareness" in which "the duality of 'subject' and 'object' simply dropped away and disappeared." Always candid, Willis acknowledges that she is still on the path, in process, and confesses, "I still find myself doing battle with the burden of guilt."

Dreaming Me is, one might say, a twenty-first-century "slave narrative" rendered in Buddhist terms. It brims over with memorable anecdotes (her meeting the Dalai Lama, who told her how to deal with policemen, and her lovely father-daughter relationship with Lama Yeshe) sprinkled along this *upasika*'s spiritual journey. In one, she realizes that the same spirit infusing Buddhism exists in Christianity as well (a nice affirmation of the truth of "dependent origination" of all things). In another, delicious story, when Willis was in Nepal, she and Lama Yeshe noticed from the upper deck of his Kopan monastery a group of Western students in the courtyard below them. "Suddenly, Lama Yeshe grabbed my arm and began calling out to all of them below. In a booming voice, he called, 'Look, all of you! Look! Look! You want to see women's liberation? *This* is'—pointing at me and patting me on the shoulders—'This *is* women's liberation! *This is* women's liberation!'"

"Let go, dear. Just let go," this gentle lama often counseled her during meditation. "The point," writes Willis, "was to let the drives and the worries go; to let the ambitions go." She admits that following this injunction, and those in the *Dhammapada*, will be a daunting challenge "for blacks and other people of color who have been historically demeaned in a world where racism still rules." After three decades of practice and teaching the history of Buddhism, her advice is simple yet profound: "When oppressive situations arise, I silently intone, 'All beings wish happiness and all seek to be free from suffering.'"

The second book, by Angel Kyodo Williams, is entitled *Being Black: Zen and the Art of Living with Fearlessness and Grace*. Like Willis, Williams feels that Buddhism offers a cure for numerous black pathologies. "It's not the way of white folks we need to get a grasp on," she writes, "it's the way of life." For this author, "Each one of our spirits suffers from the guilt of every negative image, idea, and stereotype about black people ever conceived," which creates a litany of social and spiritual woes: false cravings in the national non-culture created by capitalism; a selfish individualism that divides communities along the lines of class, skin complexion, and national ancestry; and the destabilization of relationships and families. What she urges throughout *Being Black* is

> acceptance for who we are, just as we are, whatever that may be: funky attitude, arrogant, self-pitying, too fat, kinky-haired, pimpled, freckled, too tall, too short, not enough money, always late, high-strung, unmotivated, skinny as a rail, high yellow, chinky-eyed, Kunta Kinte–looking, half-breed, flat-nosed, dim-witted, still living with your momma, working at McDonalds, conceited, know you better than anyone else, Cuchifrita, Coconut, Spic, Negro . . . So say to yourself, "Here I am, in the best way I can be at this moment." And that is all that should ever count.

Written with urgency and humor, this book's hope is to deliver to black America the tools for survival and self-transformation. Ironically, therein lies its downfall. As a poet friend remarked to me, *Being Black* tries to do too much, resulting in a congeries of well-worn Zen chestnuts. In just 192 pages, Williams gives the reader condensed, personal commentary on the Four Noble Truths, the Three Refuges, the Eightfold Path, the bodhisattva vows, the Zen ethical precepts, a chapter on how to meditate (with illustrations), a call for the American Sangha to promote diversity, and a final chapter on spiritual role models, books for further study, organizations to contact, websites to visit, and Buddhist magazines to read. Multivolume treatises have been published on any *one* of these serious, doctrinal topics. But Williams didn't want to produce either a scholarly work or even the story of one black woman's spiritual evolution. Rather, *Being Black* aspires to be a "practical," introductory, how-to handbook pitched toward "real world" black audiences, one that interprets Ch'an Buddhism in terms of the quotidian concerns, language, psychology, social problems, and "personal style" of black Americans. Williams's ambition deserves an A for effort, and her final product a C, but more importantly it raises a critical—even controversial—question for both the future of American Buddhism and a multiracial society ("Are black Americans unable to understand and accept the Dharma, or for that matter anything that originates outside their historical experience as a group, unless it is delivered with a supposedly 'black flavor'?"), which I will return to in just a moment.

Its overreachings lead *Being Black* at times to a misleading, Zen-lite interpretation of canonical principles and practices. For example, during her discussion of the Three Refuges, she blurs the distinction between the Sangha (the Buddhist community of monks, nuns, and lay followers) and the broader community of *every*one in a murky interpretation that is admirably civic-minded and all-embracing but hardly accurate. Her explication of Right Understanding (*samyag-drsti*) is also less than veridical. Furthermore, Williams errs in equating the Zen experience of "original nature" with what Westerners define as "instinct." She cannot tell the difference, in one baffling anecdote, between "mindfulness" and self-absorption. (She and a friend thoughtlessly shattered with raucous laughter the reverential silence in a church where Thich Nhat Hanh was about to speak, and Williams was offended that a woman nearby scolded her *outre* lapse from Right Speech and said, "Shhhh!"). These self-centered interpretations are of a piece with the list of activities Williams includes to help readers "Explore yourself and find the things that nourish you." Among these we find "Be at ease. Take ten very deep breaths, holding each for a few seconds before exhaling and relax in the arms of your lover."

At bottom, *Being Black* is an Oprah-style self-help manual shored up by pop Zen and a relativistic "Rashoman" vision of truth as merely perspectival. I have no problem with any of that, if it leads readers to further study, but I must point out that Williams's glancingly brief discussions of the Dharma allow her to gloss the deeply *radical* dimensions of Buddhism. What I *do* have a problem with is the condescending notion that *any* subject, Buddhism included, must be presented in a supposedly "black" style in order for black Americans to find it accessible, for there is no single, monolithic black style. That racially essentialistic belief, which is assumed from the first page of *Being Black*, is an epistemological dead end. It is refuted by black (and Hispanic) Soka Gakkai Buddhists who do not need copies of the *Lotus Sutra* written in "black English." By her own account, Jan Willis entered easily enough into *The Life of Milarepa*, thank you, without having a "hip" version of that text. For, if the truth be told, the same "letting go" of the (black) self that is the fruit of practice is also required, at least in part, for the first steps on one's journey. It is that illusory "black" self that Williams still seems attached to, and therein lies *Being Black*'s most valuable lesson for us all: Even after a lifetime of *dhyana*, and sustained periods of what Willis called "tantalizingly blissful awareness," each and every one of us can be caught by Mara's snare of ethnic dualism and vestigial Samsara.

14 | Foreword for *Nixon under the Bodhi Tree and Other Works of Buddhist Fiction*

The Ajahn would grin when he saw the cake. He would take each bite and savor it, but when the cake was gone, he would let it go.

—"In the Sky There Is No Footstep," by Margo McLoughlin

ACCORDING TO A CAUTIONARY SUTRA entitled "The Drum Peg," one of twelve talks by the Buddha in the *Opammasamutta* ("Connected Discourses with Similes"), he predicts that his teachings will be in danger of decline if monks become seduced by the sensuous beauty of art and prefer that to the Dharma. "So . . . bhikkhus," he says,

> [this] will happen with the bhikkhus in the future. When those discourses spoken by the Tathagata that are deep, deep in meaning, supramundane, dealing with emptiness, are being recited, they will not be eager to listen to them; and they will not think those teachings should be studied and mastered. But when

those discourses that are mere poetry composed by poets, beautiful in words and phrases, created by outsiders, spoken by their disciples, are being recited, they will be eager to listen to them, will lend an ear to them, will apply their minds to understand them; and they will think those teachings should be studied and mastered.

But this replacement of the teachings by lovely speech is only one side of the problematic relationship between the Buddhadharma and art. What of the danger to the artist? One of the Buddha's most poetically gifted disciples, Vangisa, felt taking pride in his Orphic creations was such a deleterious temptation, he found it necessary to take a step back from joyful outbursts that praised his teacher, examine his own mind, and then he composed these lines, which appear in the eponymous sutra, *Vangisasamyutta*:

Drunk on poetry, I used to wander
From village to village, town to town.
Then I saw the Enlightened One
And faith arose within me.

For both Vangisa and the Buddha, as well as any creator who is also a spiritual seeker, there can sometimes be a daunting challenge involved in reconciling the Path of nonattachment, desirelessness, and liberation with the enchanting yet evanescent beauty of created things. (I'm reminded of a story about Martin Luther, who once created a simple artifact—a piece of household furniture it was, or pottery, but he fashioned it so beautifully that he couldn't stop admiring his handiwork, its pleasing form, and finally had to smash it in order to free himself from attachment and his creation's spell.) So here's the question, one I've pondered and been returned to repeatedly during the more than thirty years I've devoted to trying to deliver something of Buddhist principles and insights in novels and stories like *Oxherding Tale, Middle Passage,* "China," and "Moving Pictures": how in heaven's name can a student or practitioner of the Buddhadharma *write* about nonconceptual insights that are ineffable and must be directly experienced to be authentic? Haven't centuries of Zen masters explained that language and concepts—the very stuff of stories— are themselves impediments to true awakening? How does one depict the holy? Can a fiction *about* the Buddhist experience ever be anything more than merely a finger pointing at the moon, and never the moon (or goal) itself?

Remarkably, those thorny questions are answered, and then transcended in *Nixon under the Bodhi Tree,* the world's first volume of "Buddhist fiction." I read these twenty-nine stories, each and every one, with a rare aesthetic pleasure *and* an ever-so-subtle deepening of my appreciation for such leitmotifs in Buddhist practice as suffering, impermanence, dependent origination, the status of the self as an illusion, loving-kindness toward all sentient beings, and emptiness. So many of these contemporary stories succeed as literary art, and overcome the problem the Buddha pointed out (as well as bringing a momentary quieting of our "monkey minds") precisely because *as* stories they are limpid, finely wrought fictions that never preach, never become didactic, and never proselytize. Rather, they dramatize the Dharma by taking us intimately into the lives of numerous characters, worldwide, and by faithfully exploring the very universal dilemmas each faces. Because of such attention to craft, to character and event, the writers collected in this one-of-a-kind book show us, time and again, how the Buddhist experience is simply the *human* experience, and that the transcendent can be found in the pedestrian, ordinary texture of our daily lives and doings.

Start with Gerald Reilly's O. Henry Award–winning story "Nixon under the Bodhi Tree," a powerful and moving tale of Dallas Boyd, a gay actor whose stage portrayal of America's thirty-seventh president becomes a spiritual Way. Then treat yourself to Francesca Hampton's deeply satisfying "Greyhound Bodhisattva," where a young, fallen Tibetan—"the 12th incarnation of the Pawoling Lama"—is down and out in southern California, ruined by his desire for all things American until redemption appears in the form of a drug-ravaged, tattooed young woman he meets in a bus station. Somehow, by some miracle of inspiration, Keith Heller takes us in a time machine called "Memorizing the Buddha" back to that pivotal moment two thousand years ago when the Buddha's followers decided to finally move from the oral transmission of his teachings to "convene in the cave temples at Aluvihara with our best scribes to copy out what we've memorized onto the dried *ola* leaves of the talipot palm tree," and one young man named Deva, "who had too perfect a memory," unexpectedly finds himself enlisted for this monumental project.

From the distant past you can move to the blue-collar present in Easton Waller's delightful "The War against the Lawns," and meet there both Jerry Mistretta, a boorish, ambitious man with his own lawn-mowing business, and his Cambodian helper Suchai, whose tendency to enter into *samahdi* when working leads to Thalian results—and liberation. You will meet Shakyamuni Buddha's mother, Mahamaya, before his birth in Jeff Wilson's "Buddherotica"; just maybe the Awakened One himself in a Wisconsin animal clinic, courtesy of Ira Sukrungruang's tale, "The Golden Mix"; and the spirit of a famous Japanese author (I won't tell you who or in what story).

On and on they come, an embarrassment of literary riches inventive, imaginative, and intellectually stimulating. Ironically, these accomplished, spiritually attuned writers may well find themselves with Vangisa's dilemma—the need to wrestle their prideful egos to the ground after giving us prose gifts of such perfection. That I will let them worry about in their practice. For myself, I can only say that I've waited all my life for a book like this. I feel grateful for it. And I believe you will feel the same way, too.

15 | Introduction for *Why Is American Buddhism So White?*

FOR MORE THAN TWO MILLENNIA one of the appeals of Buddhism is that happiness and freedom from suffering can be achieved by anyone, regardless of race, class, or gender. But we must remember that all convert practitioners are embodied beings who come to Dharma study from *some*where. They are firmly situated in a particular moment of history. If they are American practitioners of color, who from childhood learn to be bicultural, some portion of the real, daily suffering they experience in America will arise from racism and social injustice. And in the post–civil rights era this social suffering assumes forms that are so subtle, so deeply interwoven with our individual being-in-the-world, they are nearly invisible to white practitioners.

These unexamined, ingrained patterns of conditioning are, when viewed from a Buddhist perspective, perfect examples of what we mean by illusion if the racial or cultural self is taken to be an unchanging, enduring entity or substance. They are assumptions about identity that are as close to us as our breathing, so familiar that when these presuppositions are unveiled "awakening" to them can be experienced as deeply unsettling by practitioners who cling to a sense of "whiteness."

In the societies where Buddhism has taken root, it has adapted to the everydayness of the lives of the laity. But problems arise in a multicultural society if one racial group of practitioners, with its preferences and prejudices, has historically been privileged and dominant over others. James Baldwin explained this well when he said, "It's not the Negro problem, it's the white problem. I'm only black because you *think* you're white."

The overwhelming whiteness of American Buddhist centers is not a problem just for teachers who want to transmit the Dharma to everyone. The United States is presently undergoing a dramatic sea change. Demographers predict that by 2042 minorities collectively will outnumber whites. This "browning" of America is arguably one of the greatest cultural issues in the twenty-first century, a change that is already affecting everything from employment to popular culture, and especially our system of public education.

A recent article by Jen Graves in Seattle's *The Stranger*, entitled "Deeply Embarrassed White People Talk Awkwardly about Race," reports on how progressive whites are addressing this issue through organizations such as the Coalition of Anti-Racist Whites (CARW). Its cofounder Scott Winn acknowledges,

> Whiteness is the center that goes unnamed and unstudied, which is one way that keeps us as white folks centered, normal, that which everything else is compared to. . . . I think many white people are integrationists in that "beloved community" way, but integration usually means assimilation. . . . As in, you've gotta act like us for this to work.

And the critical race theorist Peggy McIntosh sums all this up well when she observes, "I think whites are carefully taught not to recognize white privilege, as males are taught not to recognize male privilege. I have come to see white privilege as an invisible package of unearned assets which I can count on cashing in each day, but about which I was 'meant' to remain oblivious."

In order to solve this problem, whites must listen deeply to Buddhists of color who are particularly well-suited (and perhaps even karmically directed) to take the lead in healing these wounds, not only in the American Sangha, but in the larger society as well.

16 | "We Think, Therefore We Are"

IN ONE OF THE MOST FASCINATING, thought-provoking, and scientifically grounded books on cultural relativity in recent years, the distinguished University of Michigan scholar Richard E. Nesbitt explores the dramatically different thought processes that developed over thousands of years between Westerners and East Asians. "Human cognition is not everywhere the same," he states, for some people have used different conceptual tools to understand the world.

His detailed journey into this profound (and some might feel politically incorrect) realm of difference spans history, philosophy, psychology, geography, and linguistics. His conclusions will naturally be of special interest to Western converts to Buddhism and other Eastern spiritual practices. But as Nesbitt shows through a wide range of studies, surveys, and observational research conducted by himself and his colleagues around the world, these two fundamentally different ways of conceiving and experiencing reality influence all of us, every aspect of our contemporary life—education, law, business, child-rearing, and social relation—and account for much of the misunderstanding about behavior and expectations that arises between Easterners and Westerners.

Nesbitt begins probing this description of worldviews at such variance with a historical overture of the ecological and philosophical foundations of thought in ancient Greece and China. Three characteristics are crucial hallmarks of Greek life twenty-five hundred years ago. First, "the location of the Greeks at the crossroads of the world" fed their sense of curiosity and brought this maritime, trading people into contact with different cultures to such a degree, writes Nesbitt, that "Athens itself would have been rather like the bar in *Star Wars*." Secondly, the Greeks "had a remarkable sense of personal *agency*—the sense that they were in charge of their own lives and free to act as they chose." And, lastly, "A strong sense of individual identity accompanied the Greek sense of personal agency."

This sense of agency, says Nesbitt, fueled a tradition of debate in the Greek city-state or *polis*. Debate was a spirited contest between individuals, with all the contention, dichotomies, and conflict one might expect when "persuasion by dint of rational argument" is the rule. That belief in individualism and agency also led early Greek thinkers, like Aristotle, to be "deeply concerned with the question of which properties made an object what it was" regardless of the context or field in which one might find it. "A routine habit of Greek philosophers was to analyze the attributes of an object—person, place, thing or animal—and categorize the object on the basis of its abstracted attributes." Categories are denoted by static, unchanging nouns (which Western children are taught as soon as they can talk.). This isolation of an object allowed it to be studied. Its unchanging, independent, static essence could be discovered, and none of this would have been possible without the logical principles of noncontradiction, which states that a proposition cannot be both truth and false ("A and not-A are impossible"); and the law of identity, where a thing is itself and not some other thing ("A is A regardless of the context"). Moving forward as he sketches a capsule intellectual history of the West, Nesbitt concludes that "the history of Europe . . . created a new sort of person—one who conceived of individuals as separate from the larger community and who thought in terms imbued with freedom."

The ontology underlying Asian thought is significantly different. Nesbitt argues that in contrast to the exposure the Greeks had to so many different people (and views), which led them to address contradiction in an either/or fashion, the Chinese were ethnically homogeneous and unified as a people early on. The author notes that "even today 95 percent of the Chinese population belongs to the same Han ethnic group." While the Greeks cherished agency, argued with each other in the marketplace, debated in the political assembly ("a contest between opponents"), and thought of themselves "as individuals with distinct properties, as units separate from others," the Chinese embraced *harmony* as their social ideal. "Every Chinese was first and foremost a member of a collective . . . the clan, the village, and especially the family. . . . For the early Confucians, there can be no me in isolation, to be considered abstractly: I am the totality of roles I live in relation to specific others."

In other words, Asian ontology emphasized a sense of *collective agency.* Added to that, Confucianism, with its complex network of social roles and obligations, and its "Doctrine of the Golden Mean—to be excessive in nothing and to assume that between two propositions, and between two contending individuals, there is truth on both sides," was compatible with two other great Eastern religions. One was Taoism, which teaches that "the Tao is conceived as both 'is' and 'is not'"; that "returning—moving in endless cycles—is the basic pattern of movement of the Tao"; and the interpenetration of opposites in the famous yin-yang symbol.

The other was Buddhism with its principles of the Middle Way and *pratitya samutpada* or dependent origination. The result of this fusion was that folk life reinforced a metaphysics (and vice versa) that gave priority to a "both/and" *dialectical* way of thinking, a sensitivity to interdependence, "the need to see things whole," and "the mutual influence of everything on almost everything else." Objects are not in opposition, nor are they static or unchanging. A person was "connected, fluid, and conditional," and not a "bounded, impermeable free agent." Emphasis moves to the verb (becoming), not the noun (being). For Easterners, close attention to relationships, attitudes, and the feelings of others gained in importance. Compromise and hostility resolution were highly valued. "There is a strong presumption that contradictions are merely apparent and to believe that 'A is right and B is not wrong either.' This stance is captured in the Zen Buddhist dictum that 'the opposite of a great truth is also true.'" (Think of the dialectical logic of Nagarjuna and the Madhyamika school.) And rather than abstractions, "Chinese philosophers quite explicitly favored the more concrete sense impressions in understanding the world." A wide-angle view that saw the background (field) was just as important as focusing on the figure.

Lest anyone might suspect that Nesbitt is trafficking in sweeping oversimplifications of East and West, I can assure readers that his book is filled with subtlety and nuance. He readily acknowledges, "Independence vs. interdependence is of course not an either/or matter. Every society—and every individual—is a blend of both." In his research, he finds "that it is the white Protestants among the American participants in our studies who show the most Western patterns of behavior and that Catholics and minority group members, including African Americans and Hispanics, are shifted somewhat toward Eastern patterns," and also that Continental Europeans are intermediate between East Asian and Anglo-American social attitudes and values.

But all this background is, says Nesbitt, just preparation for the heart of the book contained in chapters 4–7.

There, his studies confirm that "Westerners are the protagonists of their autobiographical novels; Asians are merely cast members in movies touching upon their lives." When the developmental psychologists Jessica Han, Michelle Leichtman, and Qi Wang studied four-to-six-year-old American and Chinese children, they found that "the proportion of self-references was more than three times higher for American children than for Chinese children. . . . American children made twice as many references to their own internal states, such as preferences and emotions, as did the Chinese children." In short, for American kids: "Well, enough about you; let's talk about me."

Figure/ground differences were confirmed when students at Kyoto and Michigan University were twice shown an underwater vignette of fish swimming. Asked what they had seen, "American and Japanese made about an equal number of references to the focal fish, but the Japanese made more than 60 percent more references to background elements including the water, rocks, bubbles, and inert plants and animals." Nesbitt provides illustrations for this experiment and another of an airport site. Taking the test myself, I discovered to my astonishment just how many obvious background details my Western-conditioned perception failed to grasp.

Nesbitt's research finds that these differences begin literally in the crib.

American mothers used twice as many object labels as Japanese mothers ("piggie," "doggie") and Japanese mothers engaged in twice as many social routines of teaching politeness norms (empathy and greetings, for example). An American mother's patter might go like this: "That's a car. See the car? You like it? It's got nice wheels." A Japanese mother might say: "Here! It's a vroom vroom. I give it to you. Now give this to me. Yes! Thank you." American children are learning that the world is mostly a place with objects, Japanese children that the world is mostly about relations.

Predictably, these subtle differences can lead to a clash of cultures. "Westerners," Nesbitt says, "teach their children to communicate their ideas clearly and to adopt a 'transmitter' orientation, that is, the speaker is responsible for uttering sentences that can be clearly understood by the hearer—and understood, in fact, more or less independently of the context. It's the speaker's fault if there is a miscommunication. Asians, in contrast, teach their children a 'receiver' orientation, meaning that it is the hearer's responsibility to understand what is being said. . . . Westerners—and perhaps especially Americans—are apt to find Asians hard to read because Asians are likely to assume that their point has been made indirectly and with finesse. . . . [They] in turn, are apt to find Westerners—perhaps especially Americans—direct to the point of condescension or even rudeness." Furthermore, Nesbitt observes, "What is intrusive and dangerous in the East is considered a means for getting at the truth in the West. Westerners place an almost religious faith in the free marketplace of ideas."

College professors such as myself occasionally see in the classroom the consequences of our aggressive, Western approach. The author includes a revealing story about Heejung Kim, a Korean graduate student at Stanford who "became exasperated with the constant demand of her American instructors that she speak up in class. She was told repeatedly that failure to speak up would be taken as an indication of failure to understand the material."

Kim put this problem to a test, having people speak out loud as they solved problems. What did her experiment find? "This had no effect on the performance of European Americans. But the requirement had very deleterious effects on the performance of Asians and Asian Americans." Nesbitt wonders, "Is it a form of 'colonialism' to demand that they perform verbally and share their thoughts with their classmates?"

Rich in examples, illustrations, both empirical studies and anecdotes, *The Geography of Thought* considers not only the differences today between East and West, but also whether there is evidence that these two cultural worlds are moving farther apart or converging. No one will see the world in quite the same way after reading it.

PART THREE

Stories

17 | Prince of the Ascetics

ONCE UPON A TIME, MY COMPANIONS and I lived in the forest near the village of Uruvela on the banks of the Nairanjana River. We were known far and wide as five men who had forsaken worldly affairs in order to devote ourselves completely to the life of the spirit. For thousands of years in our country, this has been the accepted way for the Four Stages of Life. First, to spend the spring of one's youth as a dedicated student; the summer as a busy householder using whatever wealth he has acquired to help others; the fall as an ascetic who renounces all duties at age fifty and retires into the forest; and the goal of the winter season is to experience the peace and wisdom found only in the Atma (or Self), which permeates all parts of the world as moisture seeps through sand. My brothers in this noble Fourth Stage of tranquillity, which we had just entered, were Kodananna, Bhadiya, Vappa, and Assajii. We had once been family men, members of the Vaishya (trader) caste, but now owned no possessions. We lived, as was right, in poverty and detachment. We wore simple yellow robes and fasted often. Wheresoever we walked, always in single file, Vappa, a small man with a snoutlike nose, took the lead, sweeping the ground before us with a twig broom so we would not crush any living creatures too small to see. When we did not leave our ashram to make alms rounds for food in Uruvela, we satisfied our hunger with fruit, but not taken off trees; rather we gathered whatever had fallen to the ground. Each day we wrote the Sanskrit word *ahum*, or "I," on the back of our hands so that we rarely went but a few moments without seeing it and remembering to inquire into the Self as the source of all things. People throughout the kingdom of Magadha affectionately called us *Bapu* (or father) because they knew that we had just begun the difficult path described in the Vedas and Upanishads. The scriptures say that a fast mind is a sick mind. But we, my brothers and I, were slowly taming the wild horses of our thoughts, learning the four kinds of yoga, banishing the ego—that toadstool that grows out of consciousness—and freeing ourselves from the twin illusions of pleasure and pain.

But one day it came to pass that as we made our monthly rounds in the summer-gilded village, begging for alms, the merchants and women all looked the other way when we arrived. When Assajii asked them what was wrong, they apologized. With their palms upturned, each explained how he had already given his monthly offering to a stunning young swami, a *mahatma*, a powerful *sadhu* who was only twenty-nine years old and had recently crossed the River Anoma which divided our kingdom from the land of the Shakya tribe. They said just being in his presence for a few moments brought immeasurable peace and joy. And if that were not shocking enough, some were calling him Munisha, "Prince of the Ascetics."

"How can this be?" My heart gave a slight thump. "Surely you don't mean that."

A portly merchant, Dakma was his name, who was shaped like a pigeon, with bright rings on his fingers, puffed at me, "Oh, but he *is* such. We have never seen his like before. You—*all* of you—can learn a thing or two from him. I tell you, Mahanama, if you are not careful, he will put you five lazybones out of business."

"Lazybones? You call *us* lazybones?"

"As your friend, I tell you, this young man gives new meaning to the words *sacrifice* and *self-control*."

Needless to say, none of this rested happily on my ears. Let it be understood that I, Mahanama, am not the sort of man who is easily swayed, but whatever serenity I had felt after my morning meditation was now gone, and suddenly my mind was capricious, like a restless monkey stung by a scorpion, drunk, and possessed by a demon all at the same time.

"This *sadhu*," I asked, helplessly, "where might we find him?"

Sujata, the unmarried daughter of a householder, with kind, moonlike eyes, stepped forward. "He lives at the edge of the forest by the river where the banyan trees grow. I have never seen *any* man so beautiful. Everyone loves him. I feel I could follow him anywhere . . ."

Now I was in a mental fog. There was a dull pounding in my right temple as we trekked forthwith at a fast pace back into the forest. Vappa was sweeping his twig broom so furiously—he was as angry and upset as I was—that billowing clouds of dust rose up around us, and we must have looked, for all the world, like a herd of enraged, stampeding elephants. Soon enough we tracked down the brash young man responsible for our alms bowls being empty.

To my surprise, and yet somehow not to my surprise, the villagers had not lied. We found him meditating naked, except for a garland of beads, in a diagonal shaft of leaf-filtered light from the banyan tree above him. Straightaway, I saw that his posture in meditation was perfect, his head tilted down just so, leaving only enough space that an egg could be inserted between his chin and throat. He was twenty years younger than I, his body gaunt and defined, his face angular, framed by a bell of black hair. As I glanced between his legs, I noticed that his *upastha* was twice the size of my own. He looked up when we approached, introduced ourselves, and pressed him to explain how he could have the nerve to install himself in *our* forest. In a sad, heavy way he exhaled, holding me with eyes that seemed melancholy, and said:

"I seek a refuge from suffering."

"Who," asked Bhadiya, cocking his head to one side, "are your teachers? What credentials do you have?"

"I have studied briefly with the hermit Bhagava. Then with Alara Kalama and Udraka Ramaputra, who taught me mastery of the third and fourth stages of meditation. But," he sighed, "neither intellectual knowledge nor yogic skills has yet led me to the liberation I am seeking."

I felt humbled right down to my heels. Those two venerated teachers were among the greatest sages in all India. Compared to *them*, my own guru long ago was but a neophyte on the path.

Twilight was coming on as he spoke, the blue air darkening to purple the four corners of the sky. A whiff of twilight even tinctured the shadows as he unfurled what I surmised was a bald-faced lie, a fairy tale, a bedtime story so fantastic only a child could believe it. Until a year ago, he said, he had been a prince whose loving father, Shuddodana, had sheltered him from the painful, hard and ugly things of the world. The palace in which he was raised, with its parks, lakes, and perfectly tended gardens, gave you a glimpse of what the homes of the gods must look like. He was raised to be a warrior of the Shakya tribe, had a hundred raven-haired concubines of almost catastrophic beauty, and ate food so fine and sumptuous even its rich aroma was enough to sate a man's hunger. He said he would have continued this voluptuous life of pleasure and privilege, for he had all that this world could offer, but one day while he and his charioteer Channa were out riding, he saw a man old and decrepit. On a different day he saw a man severely stricken with illness. On the third day he saw a corpse being carried away for cremation. And when he recognized that this fate awaited *him*, he could not be consoled. All satisfaction with the fleeting pleasures of his cloistered life in the palace left him. But then, on a fourth trip, he saw a wandering holy man whose equanimity in the face of the instability and impermanence of all things told him that *this* was the life he must pursue. And so he left home, abandoning his beautiful wife, Yoshodhara, and their newborn son, Rahula, and found his lonely way to our forest.

Once he had breathed these words, my companions begged to become his disciples. Kodananna even went as far as to proclaim that if all the scriptures for a holy life were lost, we could reconstruct them from just this one devoted ascetic's daily life. He had seduced them with his sincerity for truth-seeking. I, Mahanama, decided to remain with my brothers, but, to be frank, I had great misgivings about this man. He came from the Kshatriya caste of royalty. Therefore he was, socially, one *varna* (or caste) above us, and I had never met a member of royalty who wasn't smug and insensitive to others. Could only *I* see his imperfections and personal failures? How could he justify leaving his wife and son? I mean, he was not yet fifty, but he had forsaken his responsibilities as a householder. True enough, his family was well taken care of during his absence, because he was a pampered, upper-caste rich boy, someone who'd never missed a meal in his life but now was slumming among the poor, who could shave his waist-long beard, his wild hair, take a bath, and return to his father's palace if one day the pain and rigor of our discipline became disagreeable. I, Mahanama, have never had an easy life. To achieve even the simplest things, I had to undergo a thousand troubles, to struggle and know disappointment. I think it was then, God help me, that I began to hate *every* little thing about him: the way he walked and talked and smiled, his polished, courtly gestures, his refined habits, his honeyed tongue, his upper-caste education, none of which he could hide. The long and short of it was that I was no longer myself. Although I consented to study with him, just to see what he knew, I longed, so help me, to see him fail. To slip or make a mistake. Just *once*, that's all I was asking for.

And I *did* get my wish, though not exactly as I'd expected.

To do him justice, I must say our new teacher was dedicated, and more dangerous than anyone knew. He was determined to surpass all previous ascetics. I guess he was still a warrior of the Shakya tribe, but instead of vanquishing others all his efforts were aimed at conquering himself. Day after day he practiced burning thoughts of desire from his mind and tried to empty himself of all sensations. Night after night he prayed for a freedom that had no name, touching the eighty-six sandalwood beads on his *mala* for each mantra he whispered in the cold of night, or in rough, pouring rain. Seldom did he talk to us, believing that speech was the great-grandson of truth. Nevertheless, I spied on him, because at my age I was not sure any teacher could be trusted. None could meet our every expectation. None I had known was whole or perfect.

Accordingly, I critically scrutinized everything he did and did not do. And what struck me most was this: it was as if he saw his body, which he had indulged with all the pleasures known to man, as an enemy, an obstacle to his realization of the highest truth, and so it must be punished and deprived. He slept on a bed of thorns. Often he held his breath for a great long time until the pain was so severe he fainted. Week after week he practiced these fanatical austerities, reducing himself to skin and bone and fixed idea. My companions and I frequently collapsed from exhaustion and fell behind. But he kept on. Perhaps he was trying to achieve great merit, or atone for leaving his family, or for being a fool who threw away a tangible kingdom he could touch and see for an intangible fantasy of perfection that no one had ever seen. Many times we thought he was suicidal, particularly on the night he made us all sleep among the dead in the charnel grounds, where the air shook with insects, just outside Uruvela. During our first years with him he would eat a single jujube fruit, sesame seeds, and take a little rice on banana leaves. But as the years wore on, he—being radical, a revolutionary—rejected even that, sustaining himself on water and one grain of rice a day. Then he ate nothing at all.

By the morning of December seventh, in our sixth year with him, he had fallen on evil days, made so weakened, so frail, so wretched he could barely walk without placing one skeletal hand on Bhadiya's shoulder and the other on mine. At age thirty-five, his eyes resembled burnt holes in a blanket. Like a dog was how he smelled. His bones creaked, and his head looked chewed up by rats, the obsidian hair that once pooled round his face falling from his scalp in brittle patches.

"Mahanama," he said. There were tears standing in his eyes. "You and the others should not have followed me. Or believed so faithfully in what I was doing. My life in the palace was wrong. This is wrong too."

The hot blast of his death breath, rancid because his teeth had begun to decay, made me twist my head to one side. "There must be . . ." he closed his eyes to help his words along, "some Way between the extremes I have experienced."

I kept silent. He sounded vague, vaporish.

And then he said, more to himself than to me, "Wisdom is caught, not taught."

Before I could answer he hobbled away, like an old, old man, to bathe, then sit by himself under a banyan tree. I believe he went that far away so we could not hear him weep. This tree, I should point out, was one the superstitious villagers believed possessed a deity. As luck would have it, the lovely Sujata, with her servant girl, came there often to pray that she would one day find a husband belonging to her caste and have a son by him. From where we stood, my brothers and I could see her approaching, stepping gingerly to avoid deer pellets and bird droppings and, if my eyes did not deceive me, she, not recognizing him in his fallen state, thought our teacher was the tree's deity. Sujata placed before him a golden bowl of milk-porridge. To my great delight, he hungrily ate it.

I felt buoyant, and thought, *Gotcha.*

Vappa's mouth hung open in disbelief. Bhadiya's mouth snapped shut. Kodananna rubbed his knuckles in his eyes. They all knew moral authority rested on moral consistency. Assajii shook his head and cried out, "This woman's beauty, the delights of food, and the sensual cravings tormenting his heart are just too much for him to resist. Soon he will be drinking, lying, stealing, gambling, killing animals to satisfy his appetite, and sleeping with other men's wives. Agh, he can teach us nothing."

Disgusted, we left, moving a short distance away from him in the forest, our intention being to travel the hundred miles to the spiritual center of Sarnath in search of a better guru. My brothers talked about him like he had a tail. And while I cackled and gloated for a time over the grand failure of our golden boy, saying, "See, I *told* you so," that night I could not sleep for thinking about him. He was alone again, his flesh wasted away, his mind most likely splintered by madness. I pitied him. I pitied all of us, for now it was clear that no man or woman would ever truly be free from selfishness, anger, hatred, greed, and the chronic hypnosis that is the human condition. Shortly after midnight, beneath a day-old moon in a dark sky, I rose while the others slept and crept back to where we had left him.

He was gone, no longer by the banyan tree. Up above, a thin, rain-threaded breeze loosed a whirlwind of dead leaves. It felt as if a storm was on its way, the sky swollen with pressure. And then, as I turned to leave, seeking shelter, I saw faintly a liminal figure seated on kusha grass at the eastern side of a bodhi tree, strengthened by the bowl of rice-milk he had taken, and apparently determined not to rise ever again if freedom still eluded him. I felt my face stretch. I wondered if I had gone without food so long that I was hallucinating, for I sensed a peculiar density in the darkness, and the numinous air around him seemed to swirl with wispy phantoms. I heard a devilish voice—perhaps his own, disguised—demanding that he stop, which he would not do. Was he totally mad and talking to himself? I could not say. But for three watches of the night he sat, wind wheeling round his head, its sound in the trees like rushing water, and once I heard him murmur, "At last I have found and defeated you, *ahumkara*, I-Maker."

At daybreak, everything in the forest was quiet, the tree bark bloated by rain, and he sat, as if he'd just come from a chrysalis, in muted, early morning light, the air full of moisture. Cautiously, I approached him, the twenty-fifth Buddha, knowing that something new and marvelous had happened in the forest that night. Instead of going where the path might lead, he had gone instead where there was no path and left a trail for all of us. I asked him:

"Are you a god now?"

Quietly, he made answer. "No."

"Well, are you an angel?"

"No."

"Then what are you?"

"Awake."*

That much I could see. He had discovered his middle way. It made me laugh. These rich kids had all the luck. I knew my brothers and I would again become his disciples, but this time, after six long years, we'd finally be able to eat a decent meal.

* These six lines of dialogue are from the spiritual teachings of the late, great Eknath Easwaran.

18 | The Cynic

The ruler of the world is the
Whirlwind, that has unseated Zeus.
—*The Clouds,* Aristophanes

If you listen to those who are wise, the people who defended my teacher at his trial before he was killed by the state, they will tell you that the golden days of our democracy were destroyed by the war. The Corinthians, who feared our expansionist policies and growing power, convinced the Spartans to make war against us. Our leader, Pericles, knew we were stronger at sea than on shore. So he had all the inhabitants of Athenian territory in Attica huddle inside the fortifications of the city, which left the lands of the rich to be ravished by our enemies. But Pericles believed that after this sacrifice of land to the bellicose Spartans, our swift and deadly ships, triremes outfitted with three banks of oars, would wear them down in a war of attrition. His plan, this gamble, might have worked. But at the outset of the Peloponnesian War, a plague fell upon Athens, laying waste to those crowded together in the city and, if that was not bad enough, Pericles himself died the following year. With his death, power in the Assembly was seized by demagogues like the young general

Alcibiades, who convinced the voters to abandon our defensive strategies and launch an attack on the city of Syracuse in faraway Sicily. This ill-advised invasion, this poorly planned military adventure, drained the manpower and treasure of the *polis,* our city-state. Within two years of the Sicilian expedition, "the hateful work of war," as Homer might put it, had wiped out our ships and ground forces. However, this was just the beginning of the spell of chaos cast upon us by the goddess Eris.

The war dragged on for another ten years, dividing the population, feeding our disenchantment with civic life. Just as the chorus in a Sophoclean drama is powerless to stop the events leading to tragedy, so, too, no one could stop the growing hatred of the poor for the rich, or the bitterness in those wealthy families who experienced catastrophe as they lost their crops year after year. The rich began to plot against the regime, against rule by the people, and against the Assembly, which had conducted the war like a dark comedy of miscalculations and decisions based on collective self-delusion.

When our defeat finally came, after a demoralizing twenty-seven years of conflict, everyone knew this was the end of the empire, that we had unleashed the furies, and entered a time of dangerous extremes, a long-prophesied Iron Age. Crime, fraud, and violence increased. Many Hellenes started to feel that the gods like Zeus and Athena were mere fictions, or were helpless to affect our lives, and that the gossamer-thin foundation of laws and traditions our fathers and forbearers had lived by (especially our devotion to *sophrosyne,* or moderation) were arbitrary. The faith in a moral order that unified us during our Golden Age was no longer possible. It seemed that overnight loyalty to our sea-girt city-state reverted back to family, tribe, and clan, and a new breed of citizen was born. These were cold, calculating, and egotistical men like the character Jason that

Euripides created in *Medea*. They were devoted not to civic duty but instead to the immediate pleasures of food, drink, sex, and, most important of all, power. These new men, who believed might was right, like Thrasymachus, saw "justice," "honesty," and "loyalty" as ideas created by and for the weak. Not too surprisingly, a new level of nastiness, incivility, and litigation entered our lives. Of these new men, Thucydides said, "The meaning of words had no longer the same relation to things, but was changed by them as they thought proper. Each man was strong only in the conviction that nothing was secure."

Now, such new men needed new teachers, ones who were very different from the wonderful man who taught me. These teachers, foreigners, sprang up like Athena from the head of Zeus, came from places like Corinth, were called Sophists, and for a nice purse of drachmae, they instructed the children of the rich in clever rhetoric and perfumed lies aimed at appealing to the mob and swaying the members of the factious Assembly—prostitutes, my teacher called them, because he charged no fee. The most famous of these men was Protagoras, who argued that everyone knew things not as they are but only as they are in the moment of perception for *him*. "Man," he said, "is the measure of all things," and by this popular saying he meant nothing was objective, all we could have were opinions, and so each citizen was now his *own* lawgiver. (And, as you know, opinions are like assholes—everybody has one.) In my youth, then, at this hour in history, in the wreckage of a spiritually damaged society, it came to pass that common, shared values had all but vanished, truth was seen as relative to each man, if not solipsistic, and nothing was universal anymore.

Needless to say, the greatest, most unforgivable crime of my countrymen was, if you ask me, the killing of my teacher over his refusal to conform to the positions taken by different political parties. His accusers—Anytus, Meletus, and Lycon—called him an atheist, a traitor, and a corruptor of youth. Then they brought him to trial, though he could have fled the city, escaping injustice with the help of his students. Instead, and because he could not imagine living anywhere but Athens, he chose to drink the chill draught of hemlock.

To this very day, I regret that I could not be at my teacher's side when he died. That evening I was sick. But since his death, which wounded us all, I have done everything I can to honor him. Being one of his younger students, never his equal, I always feel like a son whose father has died too soon. Right when I was on the verge of maybe being mature enough to actually say something that might interest him. Sometimes I would see or hear something I wanted to share with him only to realize he was gone for the rest of *my* life. For years now I've carried on dialogues with him in my head, talking late at night into the darkness, saying aloud—perhaps too loud—all the things I wanted to tell him, apologizing for things I failed to say, often taking *his* part in our imaginary conversations until my five slaves, who are like family to me, started looking my way strangely. I didn't want anyone to think I had wandered in my wits, so I began quietly writing down these dialogues to free myself from the voices and questions in my head, adding more speakers in our fictitious conversations where his character is always the voice of wisdom, which is how I want to remember him. Yet and still, his death left scar tissue on my soul, and a question that haunts me day and night: How can good men, like Socrates, survive in a broken, corrupt society?

There was one man who seemed as bedeviled by this dilemma as I was, but his response was so different from mine. I can't say we were on the same friendly terms as Damon and Pythias, though sometimes he did feel like a brother, but one who infuriated me because he said my lectures at the Academy were long-winded and a waste of time. He was not, I confess, my only critic. My teacher's other students think my theories are all lunacy and error. They see my philosophy about eternal Ideas existing beyond the imperfections of this shadowy world as being nothing more than my cobbling together the positions of Heraclitus, who saw only difference in the world and denied identity, and Parmenides, who saw identity and denied the existence of change. In their opinion, I've betrayed everything Socrates stood for. They positively hate my political view that only philosopher-kings should rule. Antisthenes has always been especially harsh toward me, treating me as if I were as cabbage-headed as one of the residents of Boeotia, perhaps because he, and not I, was present at Socrates's side when he passed away. Years ago, he had his own school before joining ours. In his teachings he rejected government, property, marriage, religion, and pure philosophy or metaphysics such as I was trying to do. Rather, he preached that plain, ordinary people could know all that was worth knowing, that an ordinary, everyday mind was quite enough. He taught in a building that served as a cemetery for dogs. Therefore, his pupils were called *cynics* (in other words, "dog-like"), and among the most earthy, flamboyant, and, I must say, scatological of his disciples was the ascetic Diogenes.

For an ascetic, he was shamelessly Dionysian, and without an obol or lepton to his name; but besides being Dionysian and shameless, Diogenes was a clown with hair like leaves and tree bark, gnarled root-like hands, and eyes like scars gouged into stone. He made a virtue of vulgarity, wore the worst clothing, ate the plainest porridge, slept on the ground or, as often as not, made his bed in a wine cask, saying that by watching mice he had learned to adapt himself to any circumstance. Accordingly, he saw animals as his most trustworthy teachers, since their lives were natural, unselfconscious, and unspoiled by convention and hypocrisy. Like them, he was known for defecting, urinating, masturbating, and rudely breaking wind in public. He even said we should have sex in the middle of the marketplace, for if the act was not indecent in private, we should not be ashamed to do it in public. Whenever he was praised for something, he said, "Oh shame, I must be doing something wrong!" Throughout Athens he was called "The Dog," but to do him justice, there *was* a method in his madness. For example, his only possessions were his staff and a wooden bowl. But one afternoon Diogenes stumbled upon a boy using his hands to drink water from a stream. From that day forward he always drank with his bare hands and never touched his bowl again.

Thus things stood in postwar Athens when one day The Dog decided to walk around the city holding a lighted lantern. He peered into all the stalls of the marketplace, peeked in brothels, as if he had lost something there, and when asked what he was doing, replied, "I'm looking for an honest man." His quest brought him to the Academy, where I was lecturing. As I placed several two-handled drinking cups before my students, I could from the corner of one eye see him listening, and scratching at dirt in his neck seams, and sticking his left hand under his robe into his armpit, then withdrawing it and sniffing his fingers to see if he needed a bath. I sighed, hoping he'd go away. I turned to my students and told them that while there were countless cups in the world, there was only one *idea* of a cup. This idea, the essence of cupness, was eternal; it came before all the individual cups in the world, and they all participated imperfectly in the immortal Form of cupness.

From the back of the room, Diogenes cleared his throat loudly.

"Excuse me," he said. "I can see the cup, but I don't see cupness *any*where."

"Well," I smiled at my students, "you have two good eyes with which to see the cup." I was not about to let him upstage me in my own class. Pausing, I tapped my forehead with my finger: "But it's obvious *you* don't have a good enough mind to comprehend cupness."

At that point, he sidled through my students, put down his lantern, and picked up one of the cylices. He looked inside, then lifted his gaze to me. "Is this cup empty, Plato?"

"Why, yes, that's obvious."

"Then"—he opened his eyes as wide as possible, which startled me because that was a favorite trick of my teacher—"where is the emptiness that comes before this empty cup?"

Right then my mind went cloudy. My eyes slipped out of focus for a second. I was wondering how to reply, disoriented even more by the scent of his meaty dog breath and rotten teeth. And then, Diogenes tapped my forehead with *his* finger, and said, "I believe you will find the emptiness is *here*." My students erupted with laughter, some of them even clapping when he, buffoon that he was, took a bow. (That boy from Stagira, Aristotle, who was always questioning me, and expressed the preposterous belief that the ideas must be *in* things, laughed until he was gasping for breath.) "I think your teacher's problem," he told them, "is that he'd like to run away from the messiness of the world, to disappear—*poof!*—into a realm of pure forms and beauty, where everything has the order and perfection of mathematics. He's a mystic. And so—so dualistic! He actually wants certainty where there *is* none."

"What," I said, "is wrong with *that?* Things are terrible today! Everyone is suing everyone else. There's so much anger and hatred. No one trusts anyone anymore!"

Again, his eyes flew open, and he winked at my students, raising his shoulders in a shrug. "When have things *not* been terrible? What you don't see, my friend, is that there are only two ways to look at life. One is as if nothing is holy. The other is as if *every*thing is."

Oh, *that* stung.

All at once, the room was swimming, rushing toward me, then receding. I felt unsteady on my feet. In a matter of just a few moments, this stray dog had ruined my class. Now my students would always tap their heads and giggle when I tried to teach, especially that cocky young pup Aristotle. (I think he'd like to take my place if he could, but I know that will never happen.) I began to stutter, and I felt so embarrassed and overwhelmed by his wet canine smell that all I could say was, "In *my* opinion, only a fool would carry a lantern in the daytime. Why don't you use it at night like a sensible man would?"

"As a night light?" He raised his eyebrows and bugged out his eyes again. "Thank you, Plato. I think I like that."

There was nothing for me to do except dismiss my students for the rest of the day, which The Dog had ruined. I pulled on my cape and wandered through the marketplace until darkness came, without direction through the chariots, the workmen, the temples of the gods, the traders selling their wares, through helots and sun-blackened African slaves who policed our *polis,* past the amphitheater where old men prowled for young boys whose hair hung like hyacinth petals, and soldiers singing drinking songs, all the while cursing Diogenes under my breath, because the mangy cur was right. He was, whatever else, more Socratic than Socrates himself, as if the spirit of my teacher had been snatched from the Acherusian Lake, where souls wait to be reborn, and gone into *him* to chastise and correct me from beyond the grave, reminding me that I would always be just an insecure pupil intoxicated by ideas, one so shaken by a world without balance that I clung desperately to the crystalline purity and clear knowledge of numbers, the Apollonian exactitude and precision of abstract thought.

Where my theories had denied the reality of our war-shattered world, he lapped up the illusion, like a dog indifferent to whether he was dining on a delicacy or his own ordure.

Tired, I finally decided to return home, having no idea how I could summon up the courage to face my students. And it was when I reached the center of town that I saw him again. He was still holding high that foolish lantern, and walking toward me with a wild splash of a smile on his face. I wanted to back away—I was certain he had fleas—or strike him a blow for humiliating me, but instead I held my ground, and said crisply, "Have you found what you're looking for yet?"

"Perhaps," he said, and before I could step back, he lifted my chin with his forefinger and thumb toward the night sky. "What do you see?" Don't explain, *look*."

It was the first night of a full moon, but I hadn't noticed until now. Immediately, my mind started racing like that of a good student asked a question by his teacher. As if facing a test, I recalled that when Democritus tried to solve the mystery of the One and the Many, he said all things were composed of atoms, and Thales believed that everything was made of water, and Anaximenes claimed the world's diversity could be reduced to one substance, air. Oh, I could plaster a thousand interpretations on the overwhelmingly present and palpable orb above us, but at that moment something peculiar took place, and to this day I do not understand it. I looked and the plentitude of what I saw—the moon emerging from clouds like milk froth— could not be deciphered, and its opacity outstripped my speech. I was ambushed by its sensuous, singular, and savage beauty. Enraptured, I felt a shiver of desire (or love) rippling through my back from the force of its immediacy. For a second I was wholly unconscious of anyone beside me, or what was under my feet. As moonlight streamed abundantly from a bottomless sky, as I felt myself commingled with the seen, words failed me, my cherished opinions slipped away in the radiance of a primordial mystery that was as much me as it was the raw face of this full-orbed moon, a cipher so inexhaustible and ineffable it shimmered in my mind, surging to its margins, giving rise to a state of enchantment even as it seemed on the verge of vanishing, as all things do—*poleis* and philosophical systems—into the pregnant emptiness Diogenes had asked me to explain. A sudden breeze extinguished the candle inside his lamp, leaving us enveloped by the enormity of night. There, with my vision unsealed, I felt only wonder, humility, and innocence, and for the first time I realized I did not have to understand, but only to *be*.

All I could do was swallow, a gulp that made The Dog grin.

"Good." He placed one piebald paw on my shoulder, as a brother might, or perhaps man's best friend. "For once you didn't dialogue it to death. I think I've found my honest man."

19 | Kamadhatu, a Modern Sutra

The body is the bodhi tree;
The mind is like a bright mirror standing.
Take care to wipe it all the time.
And allow no dust to cling.

—Shen-hsiu

NOT FAR FROM OSAKA, DEEP IN THE forest, there is a fourteen-hundred-year-old Buddhist temple called Anraku-ji, which in Japanese means "peaceful, at ease." But the young priest who took over the care and upkeep of Anraku-ji not long ago, Toshiro Ogama was his name, felt neither truly peaceful nor at ease, and having said something as puzzling as that, it is now necessary, of course, to tell you why.

When Toshiro Ogama was fifteen, both his parents were killed in an automobile accident in Kyoto. An only child, he was suddenly an orphan. His parents' funeral, conducted by a priest in the Pure Land tradition, and their cremation were engraved into the emulsion of his memory. At the crematorium, they were incinerated at 800 degrees centigrade. Their bodies burned steadily for two hours. They had a thirty-minute cooling-down period. Finally, their bones were crushed and mixed with ashes—all total his parents each weighed two pounds at the end—and they were given back to Toshiro in two white urns. Those containers, which he kept and placed beside the altar at Anraku-ji, led him all his adult life to listen attentively whenever he heard the Buddhist Dharma or teachings. And what more? Well, he was painfully shy and, like the English scientist Henry Cavendish, he could barely speak to one person, never to two at once since four eyes looking at him made Toshiro stammer. At eighteen, he entered Shogen-ji Monastery and devoted four years to rigorous training, living on a prison diet of cheap rice and boiled potatoes in bland soup. He later passed his examinations at Komazawa University, where many Soto Zen monks have studied, but after this Toshiro decided he did not want to teach or try to work his way up through the politically treacher-ous Buddhist hierarchy and rigid, religious pecking order in Japan, which was brutally competitive, and had corrupted the Sangha, or community of spiritual seekers, by the greed and hypocrisy of the world—or at least this was what Toshiro told himself, since he was unable to speak to anyone about his real Zen fears, and why he sometimes felt like a failure, an outright fraud. Knowing he didn't have the family connections or the constitution to rise very high in the religious power structure, Toshiro chose instead to take a free-lance job translating best-selling American books for Hayakawa Shobo, a publishing company in Tokyo, and he looked around for an abandoned temple that he might repair, manage, and perhaps turn into his own private sanctuary from suffering and all the un-predictable messiness of the social world. Across Japan, there are thousands of these empty wooden buildings falling into disrepair, full of termites and rats, with tubers growing through the floor-boards, as if each was a vivid illustration of how everything on this planet was so provisional, with things arising and being unraveled in a fortnight—a fact that Toshiro had meditated on deeply, day and night, since the death of his parents.

So when he was granted permission to move into Anraku-ji, the young priest felt, at least for his first year there, a contentment much like that described by Thoreau at Walden Pond. He had no wealthy parishioners or temple supporters paying his salary. Whatever he did at the temple was voluntary, with no strings attached, paid for by his translation work, and done for its own rewards. With great care, he spent a year remodeling Anraku-ji's small main hall and adjoining house, quietly chanting to himself as he worked. He pruned branches, sawed tree limbs, and raked leaves. He trimmed bushes, did weeding and transplanting, and drifted off to sleep to the sound of crickets, bullfrogs, and an owl that each night soothed him like music. Sometimes he talked to himself as he worked, which was a great embarrassment when he caught himself doing that, so he kept a cat to have something to talk to and cover up his habit. He was alone at Anraku-ji, but not lonely, and he decided a man could do far worse than this.

Thus things stood when one afternoon a pilgrim from America arrived unannounced on the steps of his temple. This did not please Toshiro at all because, traditionally, the Japanese do not like surprises. She was a bubbly, effervescent black American about forty years old, with an uptilted nose, a smile that lit up her eyes behind her glasses, and long chestnut hair pinned behind her neck by a plastic comb. At first, Toshiro felt overwhelmed by her beauty. Then he had the uncanny feeling he should know her, but he wasn't sure why. In Japanese, he said, "*Konnichiwa*," and when she didn't answer, he said in English, "Are you lost?"

That question made her lips lift in a smile. "Spiritually, I guess I am. Aren't we *all* lost? Are you Toshiro Ogama-san?"

"Yes."

"And are you accepting students? My name is Cynthia Tucker. You're translating one of my books for Hayakawa Shobo. I would have called first, but you don't have a phone listed. I'm in Japan for a month and a half, lecturing for the State Department and—well, since I'm *here,* and have a little unscheduled time, I was hoping to meet you, and discuss any problems you might have with American words in my book, and maybe get your help with my practice of meditation." Now she laughed, taking off her glasses. "Roshi, I think I need a *lot* of help."

"I . . . I'm not a teacher," said Toshiro.

"But you *are* the abbot of this beautiful temple, aren't you?"

"Yes . . ."

"Well, if it's all right, I'd love to stay a few days and—"

"Stay?" His voice slipped a scale.

"Yes, visit with you for a while and ask a few questions." He was amused that Tucker said this while standing under the sign posted at every Zen temple and monastery, which read *Look Under Your Feet* (for the answers), but this pilgrim did not, of course, read Japanese. "I can make myself useful," she said. "And I won't be a bother. Maybe I can help you in some way, too."

As she spoke, and as he studied her more closely—her flower-patterned blouse, sandals and white slacks, how early afternoon sunlight was like liquid copper in her hair, Toshiro slowly realized that among the five books he was leisurely translating for Hayakawa Shobo there *was* one by a Dr. Cynthia Tucker, a Sanskrit scholar in the Asian Languages and Literature Department at the University of Washington. Her author's bio and American newspaper interviews with her told him she'd survived colon cancer, two divorces, had no children, taught courses in Eastern philosophy, and described herself whimsically as a Baptist-Buddhist. Her book, *The Power of a Quiet Mind,* was a hefty, three-hundred-page volume devoted to interpreting the Dharma in terms that addressed the trials and tribulations of black Americans. Toshiro was only two chapters into his translation, but he'd found her work electrifying—even culturally necessary. Her prose was incandescent, shimmering with the Right Thought of all buddhas in the ten directions, but placed within a twenty-first-century black American context. Toshiro also found this ironic. In Japan, the old ways and old wisdom had become antique after World War II. The traditions of Soto and Rinzai Zen held little interest for this younger, business-minded generation of Japanese who seemed quite satisfied pursuing the goods of the world and being salary men. But the Americans? Since the 1960s, they had become passionate about the Dharma, even when they got it wrong, and he often suspected that much of the continuation of Asian spiritual traditions might fall to them, the *gaijin* of North America who had grown weary of materialism. As much as he valued his privacy at the temple, he saw how impolite it would be to turn this very distinguished visitor away. He wasn't happy about the prospect of having to be entertaining, but it couldn't be helped. If he didn't, her publisher—his boss—would not be pleased. Even so, he had always been awkward around people and felt afraid of this situation.

The young priest brought his palms together in the gesture of gratitude and veneration, called *gasshó,* and made a quick bow.

"Forgive me for not recognizing you at first. I think your book—and *you*—are wonderful, and you *can* help me with some of the words. But I don't think you should stay for too long. One day only. I don't see people often, and I'm not such a good teacher of the Buddhadharma. Really, I don't know *any*thing."

"Oh, that's hard to believe." The corners of her eyes crinkled as she smiled. "I've read that all beings are potential Buddhas. Anyone or anything can bring us to a sudden awakening—the timbre of a bell, an autumn rose, the extinguishing of a candle. Anything!"

Toshiro's eyes slipped out of focus when she said that. She really knew her stuff, and that made his heart give a very slight jump. How would she judge him if she knew the depths of his own failure? The priest invited the pilgrim inside, offering her a cup of rice wine and a plate of rice crackers. He showed her around the temple, the two of them sometimes walking out of step in their stocking feet and bumping each other as they conversed for half the afternoon about English grammar, with Tucker sometimes placing her hand gently on his shoulder, and peppering him with questions that made Toshiro's stomach chew itself—questions like, "What time do you get up? How often do you shave your head? Is your tongue on the roof of your mouth when you meditate? Do you eat meat, Roshi? Why are Zen priests in Japan allowed to get married, but not those in China?" Toshiro noticed his palms were getting wet, and wiped them on his shirt, but his arm still tingled with pleasure where she had touched him. He excused himself, saying he needed to work a while on the stone garden he was creating. He repeated his apology, "I am the poorest of practitioners. You must ask someone else these questions. And not stay more than one night. People in the village will talk if a woman sleeps at the temple. And *don't* call me roshi."

"I understand, I'll leave." Tucker put back her head and he could feel the smile on her face going frozen. "But Ogama-san, since I've come all this way across the Pacific Ocean, please give me something to do for the temple. I insist. I want to serve. I could make a donation, but college professors don't earn very much. I'd prefer to work. I could help you in your garden."

Not wanting that, and because the words left his mouth before his brain could catch them, he told Tucker that cleaning out one of the small storage rooms at the hinder part of the main hall, which contained items left over by the temple's last abbot fifty years ago, was a chore he'd been putting off since he moved into Anraku-ji. He gave her a broom, a mop, and a pail, then Toshiro, his stomach tied up in knots, hurried outside.

For the rest of the afternoon, he pottered about in the stone garden, but he was in fact hiding from her, and wondering what terrible karma had brought this always-questioning American to Anraku-ji. He was certain she would discover that, as a Zen priest, he was a living lie. He knew all the texts, all the traditional rituals, *every*thing about ceremonial training and temple management, but he had never to his knowledge directly experienced Nirvana. He feared he would never grasp satori during his lifetime. It would take a thousand rebirths for the doors of Dharma to crack open even a little for one as stalled on the Path by sorrow as Toshiro Ogama. In Japanese, there was a word for people like him: *nise bozo*. It meant "imitation priest." And that was surely what Cynthia Tucker would judge him to be if he let her get too close, or linger too long on the temple grounds. If he were to save face, the only solution, as far as he could see, was to demand that she leave immediately.

At twilight, Toshiro tramped back to the main hall, intending to do just that. But what happened next, he had not expected. He found his visitor standing outside the storeroom, her hair lightly powdered with fine, gray dust, and heaped up around her in crates and cardboard boxes were treasures he never knew the temple contained. She had unearthed Buddhist prayers, *gatha*, written a hundred years before in delicate calligraphy on rice paper as thin as theater scrim, and wall hangings elaborately painted on silk (these were called *kakemono*) that whispered of people who had passed through the temple long before he was born—past lives that were all the more precious because they were ephemeral, a flicker-flash of beauty against the backdrop of eternity. There were also large, pewter-gray tin canisters of film, a battered canvas screen, and a movie projector from the 1950s, which Tucker was cleaning with a moistened strip of cloth. When Toshiro stepped closer, she looked up, smiling, and said, "When

I was a little girl, my parents had a creaky old projector kind of like this one. I think I can get it working, if you'd like to watch whatever is in those tin containers."

"*Yes,*" said Toshiro, "I *do.*" He picked up one of the canisters and read the yellowed label on top. "I can't believe this. These are like—how do you say?—home movies made here by my predecessor half a century ago."

Toshiro stepped aside as Tucker carried the screen and projector into the ceremony room. He plopped down on a cushion, watching her carefully thread film through sprocket wheels, test the shutter and lamp, then place the blank screen, discolored by age, fifteen feet away next to the altar. She clicked off the lights. She threw the switch, and the old, obsolete projector began to whir. There was no sound, only the flicker of images on the tabula rasa of the screen, slowly at first, each frame discrete and separated by spaces of white, as if the pictures were individual thoughts, complete in themselves, with no connection to the others—like *his* thoughts before he had his first cup of tea in the morning. Time felt suspended. But as the projector whirred on in the silent temple, the frames came faster, chasing each other, surging forward, creating a linear, continuous motion that brought a sensuously rich world to life before Toshiro's eyes. He realized he was watching a funeral in this very ceremony room, taped at Anraku-ji probably during the period of the Korean War. He felt displaced, not in space but in time. On the screen, an elderly woman lay in state, surrounded by four grieving relatives and long-stemmed white chrysanthemums. A thin blanket covered the old woman's shriveled body from her neck to her ankles. Someone had placed a small, white handkerchief over her face, and as a young man seated beside her, perhaps her eldest son, suddenly lifted the cloth and kissed her cold forehead, Toshiro felt his own face tingle and his back shiver, the experience of ruin and abandonment that overcame him during his own parents' funeral welling up inside him once again. In spite of himself, he surrendered his personal anguish, his pain—the powerful energy of his emotions—over to the people at this funeral, and this transference thickened the screen so thoroughly that the young priest's nose clogged with tears and mucus; his eyes burned with tears, but even as he sobbed uncontrollably, he knew himself to be locked in a cycle of emotion (his own) that these fleeting, black-and-white images borrowed, intensified, and gave back to him in a magic show produced by the mind, a dreamland spun from accelerated imagery. After a second, he realized this—yes, *this*—was what the sutras meant by *kamadhatu*, by the realm of illusion, by Samsara. All at once, the ribbon of film in the projector broke, returning the screen to an expanse of emptiness completely untouched by the death and misery projected upon it. For these last few moments he had experienced not the world, but the workings of his own nervous system. And this was truly all he had *ever* known. He himself had been supplying the grief and satisfaction all along, from within. Yet his original mind, like the screen, remained lotus-flower pure and in a state of grace. At that moment, Toshiro Ogama understood. He knew. He saw clearly into his own self-nature, and forever lost the sense of twoness.

Outside a breeze wuthered through yew trees and set chimes on the porch to ringing. Inside, the temple seemed to breathe, a gentle straining of wood on wood, then relaxation. Tucker clicked the lights on in the ceremony room. She saw tears streaming from Toshiro's eyes and took a step toward him. "Ogama-san? Are you alright? I didn't know this would upset you so."

He rubbed his red eyes and stood up, self-emptied. "Neither did I. Thank you for working the projector."

She gave him a fast, curious look, and then moved to where her black leather briefcase rested in a corner of the room. "I guess I'll be going now."

"Why?" said Toshiro. "In that film, I saw how once Anraku-ji was thriving with parishioners. There was a Sangha here of all sentient beings, and with no religious officials in sight. It should be that way again. Later this week I want to invite the villagers down the road to visit. Would you join my temple as its first member?"

The pilgrim did not speak, for words can be like a spider's web. She simply bowed, pressing both brown palms together in *gasshó*—one palm symbolizing Samsara, the other Nirvana—in a gesture of unity that perfectly mirrored Toshiro's own.

20 | Welcome to Wedgwood

A new Rasmussen Reports survey finds that 69% of Americans think their fellow countrymen are becoming more rude and less civilized. Men are much more likely than women to have confronted someone over their rude behavior, though more women than men think sales and service personnel are more rude than they were a decade ago. Adults over age 50 are more likely than their younger counterparts to think it is rude for someone sitting next to them in public to talk on their cell phone.

—Rasmussen Reports, August 17, 2010

I have learned silence from the talkative, toleration from the intolerant, and kindness from the unkind; yet, strange I am ungrateful to those teachers.

—Kahlil Gibran

THE TROUBLE STARTED ON A LATE afternoon in September. It was around 6:00 P.M., and I was sitting under one of the trees in my backyard, watching a brace of pigeons splash wildly around in our stone birdbath, beneath which a stone head of the Buddha rose up from the grass. My dog, Nova, a West Highland white terrier, rested peacefully nearby. I've always loved this hour of the day, when the spill of late afternoon light, so ethereal, filtered through old-growth trees in Wedgwood, a neighborhood of gentle hills and slopes at the edge of strip malls, burger joints, auto dealers, and Rich's topless nightclub in Lake City. But here you never felt you were in a big city—with all those big-city problems—because before the Second World War this area used to be an orchard filled with more apple, pear, and plum trees than people, and all that lush plumage absorbed the whoosh of traffic on Lake City Way. Here, traffic moved along at thirty miles per hour. Years ago, the neighborhood was outside the city limits, and so mailboxes were not attached to our houses but instead were out on the street, which had no sidewalks. It's been called a "prunes and raisins" neighborhood, but don't ask me why. All I know is that the spirit of place in Wedgwood (this area is named after the English china), where I've lived for half my life, was that of a quiet, hidden oasis within Seattle, inhabited mainly by older, retired people like myself, who all owned dogs, and quite a few college professors, since it was only two miles from the University of Washington. A wonderful place, if you enjoyed walking. But here and there things had begun to change. Younger people were moving in, and some years ago the police raided a home that someone had turned into a meth lab. Yet and still, such violence in Wedgwood was rare.

So that afternoon, I sat in a lazy lotus posture under an evergreen tree, the forefingers on each hand tipped against my thumbs, thinking about images from a new poem, "The Ear Is an Organ Made for Love," I'd received via email from my friend Ethelbert Miller, while behind me, floating on an almost hymnal silence, a few soothing notes sounded from the wood chimes hanging from my house, accompanied by bird flutter and the rustle of leaves at about ten decibels. Up above, the light seemed captured in cloud puffs, which looked luminous, as if they held candles within. The soughing of the wind in the trees was like rushing water. I began to slowly drift into meditation, hoping today would bring at least a tidbit of spiritual discovery, but no sooner than I'd closed my eyes and felt the outside world fall away, the air was shattered by a hair-raising explosion of music booming from stereo speakers somewhere nearby, like a clap of thunder or a volcano exploding. Now, I love music, especially soft jazz, but only at certain, special hours of the day. This was heavy-metal techno-pounding at 120 decibels, alternating with acid rock, and sprinkled with gangster rap that sounded to my ear like rhymed shouting. And it *did* rock—and shock—the neighborhood with a tsunami of inquietude. Its energy was five billion times greater than that from the wood chimes. It compressed the air around me and clogged my consciousness. I looked at Nova, and behind his quiet, blackberry eyes he seemed to be thinking, "What is *that,* boss?"

"Our new neighbors," I said. "We haven't introduced ourselves to them yet, but I guess they're having a party."

You have to understand, I talk to my dog all the time, which is better than talking to myself and being embarrassed if someone caught me doing that, and he never says a word back, which is no doubt one of the reasons why people love dogs.

One or two hours went by, and we listened helplessly as the exhausting, emotionally draining sound yeasted to 130 decibels, moving in concentric spheres from my neighbor's place, covering blocks in every direction like smog or pollution or an oil spill, and just as toxic and rude, as enveloping and inescapable as the Old Testament voice of God when He was having a bad day. And now, suddenly, *I* was having a bad day. This was exactly the opposite of the tranquillity I wanted, but there was no escaping the bass beat that reverberated in my bones, the energy of the shrill profanity and angry lyrics as they assaulted the penetralia of my eardrums, traveling down to the tiny, delicate hairs of the cochlea, and from there to the sensitive, sympathetic nervous system that directed the tremors straight into my brain. Unlike an unpleasant vision, from which I could turn away or close my eyes, wave upon wave of oscillations passed right through my hands when I held them against the sides of my head. The music, if I may call it that, was intrusive, infectious, wild, sensual, pagan, orgasmic, jangling, indecent, and filled me with foreign emotions not of my own making, completely overwhelming and washing away my thoughts and the silent, inner speech we all experience when our soul talks to itself.

I no longer recognized Wedgwood as my neighborhood. All its virtues—the magnificent views of Lake Washington and the Cascade Mountain range, its old-world charm—had vanished, and I felt as if I'd been suddenly teleported to Belltown at 11:00 P.M. on a Saturday night. I wondered if the Generation X new arrivals to the neighborhood knew how fragile our ears are, and how many scientific studies indicated that noise pollution interfered with learning, lowered math and reading scores, and was responsible for high blood pressure, dry mouth, blindness, muscular contractions, neurosis, heart disease, peptic ulcers, constipation, premature ejaculation, reduced libido, insomnia, congenital birth defects, and even death.

Now darkness had fallen, but still the pulsions continued across the street, surrounding my house like a hand squeezing a wineglass on the verge of shattering. My brain was beginning to feel like one long smear on the inside of my skull. I shook my head at the thought of what a dangerously noisy species we humans are with our clanking, humming, churning machinery and motorcars, our loud music and household appliances with their anapestic beat, and fire sirens wailing. Walking into the house, I saw my wife coming down the stairs, wearing her round reading glasses and looking dazed. At sixty-two, she was slightly hard of hearing in one ear, but the stramash had shaken and made her feel exiled from the familiar, too. She started shutting all our windows. But that didn't help. The sound curdled the air inside our house, and her sore ears were burning as badly as mine. From the porch we could see cars lining the street, beer cans thrown into the bushes, and from our neighbor's property there wafted pungent clouds of Purple Haze and Hawaii Skunk marijuana.

"I was reading the Book of Psalms in bed," my wife said, "but I couldn't concentrate with all that noise. What do you think we should do?"

"Call nine-one-one?"

"Oh, no!" she said. Unlike Nova, she *did* talk back to me. "They're just kids. We were kids once, remember? " Then suddenly her lips pouted and she looked hurt. "Why are you shouting at me?"

"Was I shouting?"

"Yes," she said. "You were yelling at me."

I didn't realize how much I'd raised my voice in order to be heard over the mind-blinding music blaring outside—she was, after all, only two feet away from me. Or that the noise, despite all my decades of spiritual practice, could so quickly make me feel spent and flammable and reveal an irascible side of me to my wife neither of us had seen in forty years of marriage. Now I felt unsure of myself, though I suspected this was a teachable moment, as politicians say, and there was a lesson to be learned here—but, so help me, I just wasn't getting it. I apologized to my wife. I knew she was right, as usual. We shouldn't call the police. This was a difficult situation that had to be handled with delicacy, but I was confident that I could be as magnanimous and civilized as any post-Enlightenment, Western man who had control over himself after thirty years of meditation on his mushroom-shaped cushion. But that didn't mean I couldn't try to escape for a while.

I decided this was a good time to go shopping. I stepped outside, where the rough, pounding sound almost knocked me to my knees. The traumatizing waves were so thick I felt I was moving through a haze of heat, or underwater. I wondered, who *are* these rude people? These invaders? I strapped Nova into my Jeep Wrangler and, with my wife's long list of groceries in the hip pocket of my jeans—milk, canned vegetables, paper towels, a chocolate cake to celebrate the birthday of one of her friends at Mount Zion Baptist Church, and dog treats—we fled into the night or, more precisely, to the QFC on 35th Avenue.

As the Doppler effect kicked in, as I put half a mile between myself and Ground Zero, as the pitch declined, I felt less agitated, though there was a slight ringing and seashell sound in my ears, lingering like a low-grade fever. For all the discomfort I was feeling, I also felt something else: namely, how sound and silence, so universal in our lives as to normally be ignored, were profound mysteries I'd never properly understood or respected until now when the absence of one and the presence of the other was so badly disrupting my life.

Compared to my street, the supermarket, surrounded by eateries and alehouses, was mercifully quiet. I went down the aisles, collecting items we needed, remembering that just one month ago, a QFC employee charged with domestic violence for choking his mother unconscious was killed in this supermarket when he fought the police who came to arrest him. I kept thinking, as I picked items off the shelves, *Are those vibes still in this store?* (You can probably tell I came of age in the sixties.) I dismissed that thought, and then stood patiently in the checkout line behind five other customers, one being a plump, elderly woman with frosted hair who, of course, had to pay by writing a check, which seemed to take forever. I swear, I think she was balancing her checking account or calculating her quarterly taxes, there at the front of the line. I could imagine her drinking a hot cup of Ovaltine before going to bed and having ninety-seven cats in her mid-century Wedgwood home. I kept wondering why someone didn't call for another cashier—or even better, two—to handle this line of people backed up into the aisles. Finally, after ten minutes it was my turn. The cashier was a genial, young man whose eyes behind his wire-framed glasses looked glazed from ringing up so many customers, but he was trying to be cheerful. He took my QFC Advantage card, and said, "So how is *your* day going?"

Usually, I enjoy chatting with people behind the cash register, finding out a little about their lives, letting them know they're people in my community I care about and not just faceless objects to me. I try to be patient, reciting my mantra if I have a long wait in a public place. But right then I said, in spite of myself, "What the hell do you care?"

That reply shocked him as much as it did me. I tried to recover. I said, "Sorry! I didn't *mean* that. I think I'm vibrating too fast."

He cut his eyes my way. "Excuse me?"

"Long story . . . Never mind."

"You want paper or plastic?"

My voice wobbled. "Paper . . . please."

That would prove to be a mistake.

Then I hurried out of QFC, pushing my little gray cart with four bags of groceries as quickly as I could, and stopped at Rite-Aid across the street to buy earplugs for my wife and myself. It was now 9:30 P.M. Driving home, I was praying the neighbor's party was over, but I felt, even though my ears were plugged, the density in the schizzy air before I heard the humping arcs still flooding the neighborhood like a broken water main. Even worse, when I downshifted into my driveway, I had to hit the brakes because another car was parked in *my* space. My neighbor's guests had filled the street with their vehicles. The one in my driveway, a Chevrolet Blazer, had a skull-and-bones decal in the back window, and under that a bumper sticker that said *You Can Kiss The Crack Below My Back.* My first impulse was to let the air out of its tires, but then I realized that would only keep it in my driveway even longer.

So I parked two blocks away. I looped Nova's nylon leash around my left wrist, loaded up my arms as high as my chin with four heavy bags of food, and started tramping slowly uphill back to my house. That's when fat raindrops began to fall. By the time I was thirty feet from my front door, the paper bags were soaking wet and falling apart. Ten feet from the front door, Nova realized we were almost home. He sprang forward for the steps—Westies hate to get wet—and that snapped my left arm straight out, which sent cans of sliced pineapples, soup and tomatoes, bottles of maple syrup and milk, and bags of raisins, potatoes, and rice cascading back down the declivity, littering the street like confetti or a landfill. For the longest time, I stood there, head tipped and sopping wet, watching my neighbor's guests flee inside to escape the rain, lost in the whorl of violent, invisible vibrations, and I was disabused forever of the vanity that three decades of practicing meditation had made me too civilized, too cultivated, too mellow to be vulnerable to or victimized by fugitive thoughts—anger, desire, self-pity, pettiness—triggered in me from things outside. These would always arise, I saw, even without noise pollution.

Then, all at once, the loud music stopped.

Dragging my dog behind me, I slogged across the street, so tired I couldn't see straight. I climbed my new neighbor's stairs, and banged my fist on the front door. After a moment it opened, and standing there with a can of Budweiser in his right hand was possibly the most physically fit young man I'd ever seen. I placed his age at thirty. Maybe thirty-five. In other words, he was young enough to be my son. His short hair was a military buzz cut, his T-shirt olive-colored, his ears large enough for him to wiggle if he wanted to, like President Obama's, and on his arm I saw a tattoo for the Fourth Brigade of the Second Infantry Division he'd served with at Fort Lewis-McChord. He looked me up and down as I stood dripping on his doorstep, and politely said:

"Yes, sir? Can I help you?"

"We need to talk," I said.

He squinted his eyes as if trying to read my lips. Then he put one hand behind his ear like an old, old man who'd lost his hearing aid, or someone who'd been a blacksmith all his life. "What did you say, sir?"

I was less than a foot away from him. I felt like I was coming to from a dream. A profound sadness swept over me, dousing my anger, for I understood the unnecessary tragedy of tinnitus in someone so young. His was maybe the result of a recent tour in Iraq or Afghanistan, perhaps from an IED. I felt humbled. I did not judge him or myself now, because he had taught me how to listen better. I gestured with one finger held up for him to wait a moment, and went back out into the downpour. On the street, I found the one item, protected by a plastic lid, that had not been ruined by the rain. I climbed the steps again.

"Thank you," I said, giving him the chocolate cake. "And welcome to Wedgwood."

21 | Guinea Pig

I was a student at the University of Washington in Seattle, with a double major in philosophy and English, those two broken and declining (if not already dead) fields in higher education, and by the end of my third year I was going broke and couldn't afford both tuition and food, but because I was physically healthy (mentally is a different matter), I started selling my vital fluids to the blood bank and volunteering for every science experiment conducted on campus, and even off-campus by aspiring inventors, provided they paid the participants.

So instead of preparing for my classes this fall, I'm sitting in a chair middlemost a laboratory longer than it is wide, lit overhead by soft fluorescent bulbs beneath one of the science buildings funded by the Bill and Melinda Gates Foundation. Their largess is visible everywhere on campus, but especially here in the high-tech labs and über-state-of-the-art scientific equipment. Miles of cables like a nest of boa constrictors are hidden away behind the walls, ceiling, and floor. Flasks and burners in the lab are interspersed with a warren of monitors, scanners that in seconds can read every chemical beneath the casement of your skin, then spit forth a fire hose of data into devices that compute a thousand times faster than human thought. Two technicians of twenty-five and thirty, very polite, are making last-minute adjustments. I've been calling them Alphonse and Gaston, because one is tall with a stiff, sliding way of walking, while the other is bald, has a belly that bubbles over his belt, and keeps a goofy little grin plastered on his face.

In the middle of this elaborate machine, this triumph of the Enlightenment, on a rainy evening in October, we're waiting for Dr. Samantha Conner to signal the start of her experiment, and on the brink of being bushwhacked by X-rated revelations no stuffy philosophy seminar can provide. I'm guessing she is thirty-five, a workaholic, single, the sort of brainy woman who won prize after prize at science fairs in middle school, a child prodigy who skipped high school, started at MIT when she was thirteen, earned a MacArthur Fellowship before she was old enough for a driver's license, and had no time for something as frivolous as boys or dating because she still had to prove herself over and over in the higher echelons of the rigorous hard sciences where members of her gender are too few and far between. For me, a lowly, financially ludicrous philosophy geek in the unscientific, subjective world of literary studies, Dr. Conner, as she studies some head-breaking equation on her clipboard, is so heartbreakingly beautiful she makes my eyes blur, like maybe I'm looking at Gwyneth Paltrow in a white lab coat, gold-framed oval glasses over leaf-green eyes, with fawn-like ears, a nose turned up at the tip, and copper-colored hair spilling across her shoulders. I guess I've always had a serious case of slide-rule envy. Cerebral women with IQs over 170 have always been catnip for me, the way mountain climbers are drawn to the Matterhorn. I just fall apart in their presence. And I knew my desire for her was not just painful but also impossible. By the way the world reckoned things, I was a loser headed for the night shift at McDonald's. ("Would you like fries with that and a definition of *agape?*") Microsoft didn't need a resident metaphysician. And a bachelor's degree in English was about as good as one in basket-weaving. Nevertheless, I had a theory that all those messy, bottled-up feelings and the wild, sensual joy celebrated in the sloppy humanities, but repressed in the sciences by quantification and reducing everything to the clarity of numbers, just might under the right conditions explode like a truckload of Chinese fireworks.

During my interview, my heart did get ahead of me. I asked Dr. Conner if she'd have dinner with me at Faire Gallery Café on Capitol Hill, despite the differences in our ages, bank accounts, and academic rank. The blistering stare she gave me, peering over the rim of her spectacles, was paralyzing, like maybe I was something toxic she was looking at in a petri dish—English and philosophy majors get this kind of Godzilla-eyeball all the time.

I told her, "I'm a lot smarter than you think."

"You'd have to be," she said, spanking me for taking such liberties above my station.

Cold and efficient, she avoided my romantic overture. But I could sense how important this new study would be for her career. She said it was based on work conducted in 2008 at the Karolinska Institute in Stockholm by Valeria Petkova and her colleague Henrik Ehrsson. These two called it the "body-swap illusion." Their test subjects wore a shiny, black helmet that favored ones used in football minus the face guard, and sat across from another person or a mannequin like the crash dummies used to test air bags in cars, and after just a few moments of being rigged up like that, they shook hands and experienced the mind-warping sensation that they had suddenly switched bodies with those Others. In a word, the illusion was that they were lifted out of themselves, however briefly, freed from the tight Cartesian cage that always held the self cloistered, locked in solitary confinement as a lonely monad forever separate from other unreachable monads—as I was from Samantha Conner—ontologically isolated, solipsistic, drifting through life with the rest of the world, its objects and others, always "over there." Their work promised to be a new tool for exploring that greatest of all mysteries, self-identity; for breaking down the epistemological apartheid of mind-body dualism; and for enhancing virtual reality experiences.

But here's the trick:

Dr. Conner and her technicians won't use a lifeless mannequin. Or even another person. No, she dismissed that as being too easy. Too tame. She told me she had always been a nonconformist, an explorer always in pursuit of the extraordinary, a person who questioned authority and rejected any rules that held women back in a patriarchal society. Since childhood, Samantha had always looked at familiar things as if they were strange, and strange things as if they were familiar. She was congenitally disposed to always challenge conventions, the pedestrian, the predictable, the mundane, and going where others feared to go. I swear, her spirit of adventure and imagination stirred me up like music. Because she tilted toward innovation and breaking taboos (and also because, to my knowledge, she hadn't published a scientific paper in five years), she said my companion in her raising the stakes on Petkova's study would not even be human.

He's sitting right in front of me now, a 130-pound Rottweiler named Casey. Her dog: lazily licking its paws, and wearing a black helmet just like the one I'm holding in my hands. It covers his eyes and pointed ears, and displays a 3-D version of what the other participant sees. In other words, what *I* see. I wasn't surprised that she was uncommonly fond of her dog and selected him to be my partner. People in Seattle are so in love with this species they probably spell its name, dog, backwards, and why not? Canines and humans have a 75 percent overlap between their genetic codes.

From one of my seminars on Plato's *Republic*, I remembered that in book 2 Socrates praised dogs for being high-spirited lovers of wisdom. So, yeah, I was OK with dogs, that symbol of fidelity. But I'm wondering, you know, how all this is going to turn out, if maybe I should have told her about some of the other, bizarre experiments for which I'd been a human guinea pig, if maybe all *that* might somehow prove to be an X factor neither she nor I had figured on. Maybe when I signed the consent form, which elaborated on the possible side effects of this experiment, but also pointed out that some consequences were unpredictable and might cause death, maybe I should have told her then in that tiny office of hers, with a wall of awards, the sawdust smell of new books, and a view of Lake Washington, that some of those government-funded studies I survived won or were finalists for the Ig Nobel Prizes handed out for the most ridiculous scientific research conducted every year.

Over a period of two years, I participated in experiments that measured people's brainwave patterns while they chewed different colored M&Ms. In another experiment I was tested to determine if University of Washington males were more sexually attracted to UW females than to tennis balls—we were, according to the findings, but only marginally. I was the test subject for a musical condom that contained a microchip like the ones in musical greeting cards—when used it played the "1812 Overture" and Handel's "Messiah." And I will never forget the bumps I got on my head from a study called "Injuries Due to Falling Coconuts"; or the survey I was in about human belly button lint—who gets it, when, what color, and how much.*

---

* Examples of Ig Nobel prize winners are taken from *The Ig Nobel Prizes: The Annals of Improbable Research* by Marc Abrahams (New York: Dutton, 2002). Dog facts are from Stephen Budiansky's *The Truth about Dogs* (New York: Penguin, 2000) and Stanley Coren's *How Dogs Think* (New York: Free Press, 2004).

"Jeremy," said Dr. Conner, tapping the end of her nose with a pencil." Are you ready?"

"Yes, ma'am," I sat up straight in my chair. "I think so."

The shiny, plastic helmet was as light as Styrofoam in my hands. It would cover everything except my mouth. Slowly, I slid it over my head, plunging the room into darkness as black as onyx. I could faintly hear voices around me, Dr. Conner and her two technicians, but the world was void, without form or light for the longest time, as it must have been in the nanoseconds before the Big Bang. So far all right. I felt Alphonse throw a switch on the side of my helmet. It began to hum. But then, unbeknownst to the others, some kind of circuit went haywire. Inside the helmet my nostrils caught a whiff of smoke, then pain like a burning wire stabbed through my temples. I winced, and held my breath, but I didn't let on that anything might be wrong. I wanted full payment for my participation in this, so I didn't want them to terminate it prematurely.

Gradually and by degrees, the pain subsided. On the screen inside my helmet I began to see spicules of light, but I was color-blind. I could only see things sharply if they were about a foot away. The character of the lab had changed into a soft-focus watercolor of washed-out blues and pale yellows, as if everything was covered by a diaphanous piece of cellophane smeared with Vaseline. But what I was suddenly lacking now in depth of field was more than compensated for by the tone-color of all that I could smell angling across the air—Gaston, I realized, had a few recreational drugs and a dime bag of cannabis in his lab coat (the excellent herb called Hawaii Maui Wowie), which I guess explained why he was always grinning; and Alphonse, whether he knew it or not, was carrying in his wallet fives, tens, and twenties scented with just a trace of cocaine, which can be found on nine out of ten bills in the United States. Then, as I turned my head,

I saw a hazy, helmeted shape, larger than myself, hairless (which struck me as very odd), and wearing a white T-shirt emblazoned with the slogan *Consciousness: That Annoying Time Between Naps.* It was a totally ridiculous-looking, two-legged creature without a tail, chicken-necked, with thin, unmuscled arms, not good for anything, as far as I could see, except maybe rubbing your tummy or opening doors so you could go outside. Only at that instant did I realize it was me seen from Casey's side of the room. Not just through the camera in his helmet, but through the exotic difference of his mind as he experienced the roomscape as an explosion of odors sweet and pungent, subtle and gross, moist and dry, everything elemental, not lensed through language, not weakened by a web of words, not muddled by culture or cultivation. I heard a collage of sounds I could pinpoint the location for in one eighteen-thousandth of a second, sounds four octaves higher than humans can perceive: the world as it might be known to an extraterrestrial from the Zeta Reticuli star system. Then Dr. Conner said, "Go ahead you two, Jeremy, Casey, shake hands."

When I lifted then planted what felt like my black-padded paw in the palm of whoever that pathetically deaf, nose-dead creature was over there, when I touched myself touching, I was completely in Casey's body, he in mine: two entangled electrons. All at once, the world became new, a place of mystery and the uncanny, the way a two-year-old sees it, and strangest of all was my knowing there had to *already* be a bit of the canine in me, and the *Homo sapien* in Casey, for the experiment to work in the first place. The doctor was more successful than she knew. For just this moment, not only did it feel like we'd switched bodies, but our minds had commingled, too.

And then, as abruptly as it began, the experiment was over.

I felt Gaston lifting off my helmet. For an instant the light in the lab blinded me. I kept blinking and saw through fluttering eyelids Dr. Conner leaning toward me, using one finger to push her glasses higher on her nose toward her glabella.

"How do you feel?" she said. "Describe what happened."

I wasn't sure I could. Yes, the body-swap illusion was over. But having been freed from my skin, after stepping outside a fixed idea of myself, I couldn't exactly find my way back in, as if inside and outside, here and there, had always been the real illusion and I just never noticed it before now. Thanks to Dr. Conner's experiment, I could no longer tell, in terms of the big picture, where I ended and others began.

Can you?

Yet, she and the technicians still *did* look faintly like a different species to me, as strange as snakes or snails. Involuntarily, I started scratching myself. And for some reason I felt more cagey, manipulative, and as playful as a puppy.

"It worked just like you said it would," I told her. "Just like it did at the Karolinska Institute. You know, I think you're going to get a Nobel Prize."

"Really? You do?" Her eyes crinkled at the thought, and that wrinkled her nose. "Why?"

"Well, there was some kind of short in the helmet's circuitry, and—and even before we shook hands, the switch happened, I mean it *really* happened, not with our bodies, but our thoughts."

"Thoughts? That's not possible," she said. "Can you prove that?"

"OK." I drew a deep breath. "Just before you turned things off, I got an image from Casey, evanescent but a clear picture in my mind . . ."

"Of what?"

"Does your bedroom have a print of Picasso's *Three Musicians* on the wall, over the bed?"

"Yes."

"And a blue corduroy bedspread?"

Her eyebrows rose. "Yes, I bought that last year."

"And you listen to George Clinton music on your iPod?"

"Yes—yes, I do." She cut her eyes at me. "Jeremy, where is this going?"

"Well, I saw you on that bed. George Clinton's 'Atomic Dog' was playing. Some nights you let Casey sleep close by in the corner. And you always sleep in the buff. You've got the cutest mole on your abdomen, and this really great honey-pot tattoo on the upper, inner part of your left thigh . . ."

Dr. Conner cupped her right hand over my mouth. I'd never seen anyone move so quickly. Alphonse and Gaston looked round at her in wonder. The doctor's cheeks flushed cherry pink.

"That's just a carryover from college and too many margaritas one night," she laughed, her voice quivering. "I think Jeremy may need to rest awhile. Why don't you two take a coffee break."

I pulled her hand down, and said, "No, I'm fine. I like to sleep in the buff, too. And then there's that *other* tattoo on—"

Samantha's clipboard fell clattering to the floor, and she hissed at Alphonse and Gaston, "Leave. *Now!*"

They hurried out of the room, and when she swung her head back toward me, I was so mesmerized by the beauty of the golden highlights in her hair that, in spite of myself, a new impulse took hold of me.

I licked her face.

That sent her backpedaling about five feet, holding the wet spot as if she'd been stung. And now she had a spot of lipstick on her front tooth. After a moment, Samantha composed herself. She smoothed down her black skirt, picked up her clipboard, found her pencil, and was again the portrait of professionalism, taking notes in her obsessively neat and idiosyncratic script, her

T's like the Space Needle, her *M*'s like an outline of the Cascades.

"Is there anything *else*, Jeremy?" Her eyes were evasive. "These perceptual and behavioral transformations are, um, unprecedented. I want to know everything."

Actually, she did not want to know *every*thing, so I thought it best not to tell her that, like Casey, I had an overwhelming urge to sniff her butt, something of which she did not approve, of course, but in his case and mine it was just in the disinterested pursuit of gathering information, you understand.

"Oh, there's a lot more," I said. "You're going to have enough new research for publications to last a lifetime. Naturally, I'm at your service for any further experiments, conferences, or lectures you'll be called upon to do. You know, as living proof of your success with interspecies communications. I can also help you translate technical jargon into proper English, which will make your research reader-friendly for a larger, public audience, especially with dog lovers. That means more popularity for you and easier fund-raising. You might even need to start an institute. But sorting all this out will take a while. I'd say days. Even weeks or years. Maybe we can start by you letting me take you to dinner." I was still trying to bridge the gap between the arts and sciences.

I saw her shoulders relax. She lowered her clipboard to her side, and experimented with a smile. Just as I was seeing things anew, I could tell by the tilt of her head that she was perhaps seeing Jeremy Tucker, English and philosophy major, for the first time.

"So much about you *is* different now," she said. "You seem much more useful and . . . *feral*. Yes, I think perhaps we can do dinner. I'll bring a tape recorder."

I figured we had enough to discuss for a lifetime, and who knows where things might go from there? But this is where my fabliau (I believe that's the right form; I aced a class on the genre) ends, one I hope caused no offense, but if it did, try to keep in mind that sometimes every able-bodied American male enjoys being a dog.

22 | The Weave

IEESHA IS NERVOUS AND TRYING NOT to sneeze when she steps at four in the morning to the front door of Sassy Hair Salon and Beauty Supplies in the Central District. After all, it was a sneeze that got her fired from this salon two days ago. She has a sore throat and red eyes, but that's all you can see because a ski mask covers the rest of her face. As she twists the key in the lock, her eyes are darting in every direction, up and down the empty street, because we've never done anything like this before. When she worked here, the owner, Frances, gave her a key so she could open and straighten up the shop before the other hairstylists arrived. I told her to make a copy of the key in case one day she might need it. That was two days ago, on September first, the start of hay fever season and the second anniversary of the day we started dating.

Once inside the door, she has exactly forty seconds to remember and punch in the four-digit code before the alarm's security system goes off. Then, to stay clear of the motion detectors inside that never turn off, she gets down on the floor of the waiting room in her cut-knee jeans and crawls on all fours past the leather reception chairs and modules stacked with copies of *Spin, Upscale,* and *Jet* magazines for the salon's customers to read and just perhaps find on their glossy, Photoshopped pages the coiffure that is perfect for their mood at the moment. Within a few seconds, Ieesha is beyond the reception area and into a space, long and wide, that is a site for unexpected mystery and wonder that will test the limits of what we think we know.

Moving deeper into this room, where the elusive experience called beauty is manufactured every day from hot combs and cream relaxers, she passes workstations, four on each side of her, all of them equipped with swiveling styling chairs and carts covered with appliance holders, spray bottles, and Sulfur8 shampoo. Holding a tiny flashlight attached to her key ring, she works her way around manicure tables, dryer chairs, and a display case where sexy, silky, eiderdown-soft wigs, some as thick as a show pony's tail, hang in rows like scalps taken as trophies after a war. Every day the customers at Sassy Hair Salon and the wigs lovingly check each other out for some time, and then after long and careful deliberation, the wigs always buy the women. Unstated, but permeating every particle in that exchange of desire, is a profound, historical pain, a hurt based on the lie that the hair one was unlucky enough to be born with can never in this culture be good enough, never beautiful as it is, and must be scorched by scalp-scalding chemicals into temporary straightness, because if that torment is not endured often from the tender age of even four months old, how can one ever satisfy the unquench-able thirst to be desired or worthy of love?

The storage room containing the unusual treasure she seeks is now just a few feet away, but Ieesha stops at the station where she worked just two days ago, her red eyes glazing over with tears caused not by ragweed pollen but by a memory suspended in the darkness.

She sees it all again. There she is, wearing her vinyl salon vest, its pockets filled with the tools of her trade. In her chair is an older customer, a heavy, high-strung Seattle city council-woman. The salon was packed that afternoon, steamed by peo-pled humidity. A ceiling fan shirred air perfumed with the odor of burnt hair. The councilwoman wanted her hair straightened, not a perm, for a political fund-raiser she was hosting that week. But she couldn't—or wouldn't—sit quietly. She kept gossiping nonstop about everybody in city government as well as the do Gabby Douglass wore during the Olympics, blethering away in the kind of voice that carried right through you, that went inside like your ears didn't have any choice at all and had to soak up the words the way a sponge did water. All of a sudden, Ieesha sneezed. Her fingers slipped. She burned the old lady's left earlobe. The councilwoman flew from her seat, so enraged they had to peel her off the ceiling, shouting about how Ieesha didn't know the first thing about doing hair. She demanded that Frances fire her. And even took things a step farther, saying in a stroke of scorn that anyone working in a beauty salon should be looking damned good herself, and that Ieesha didn't.

Frances was not a bad person to work for, far from it, and she knew my girlfriend was a first-rate cosmetologist. Even so, the owner of Sassy Hair Salon didn't want to lose someone on the city council who was a twice-a-month, high-spending customer able to buy and sell her business twice over. As I was fixing our dinner of Top Ramen, Ieesha quietly came through the door of our apartment, still wearing her salon vest, her eyes burning with tears. She wears her hair in the neat, tight black halo she was born with, unadorned, simple, honest, uncontrived, as genuinely individual as her lips and nose. To some people she might seem as plain as characters in those old-timey plays, Clara in Paddy Chayevsky's *Marty* or Laura Wingfield in *The Glass Menagerie*. But Ieesha has the warm, dark, and rich complexion of Michelle Obama or Angela Bassett, which is, so help me, as gorgeous as gorgeous gets. Nevertheless, sometimes in the morning, as she was getting ready for work, I'd catch her struggling to pull a pick through the burls and kinks of her hair with tears in her eyes as she looked in the mirror, tugging hardest at the nape of her neck, that spot called the "kitchen." I tell her she's beautiful as she is, but when she peers at television, movies, or popular magazines where generic blue-eyed, blonde Barbie dolls with orthodontically perfect teeth, Botox, and breast implants prance, pose, and promenade through the media, she says with a sense of fatality and resignation, "I can't look like that." She knows that whenever she steps out our door, it's guaranteed that a wound awaits her, that someone or something will let her know that her hair and skin will never be good enough, or tell Ieesha her presence is not wanted. All she has to do is walk into a store and be watched with suspicion, or have a cashier slap her change on the counter rather than place it on the palm of her outstretched hand. Or maybe read about the rodeo clown named Mike Hayhurst at the Creston Classic Rodeo in California who joked that "*Playboy* is offering Ann Romney $250,000 to pose in that magazine and the White House is upset about it because *National Geographic* only offered Michelle Obama $50 to pose for them."

Between bouts of blowing her nose loudly into a Kleenex in our tiny studio apartment, she cried that whole day she got fired, saying with a hopeless, plaintive hitch in her voice, "What's wrong with me?" Rightly or wrongly, she was convinced that she would never find another job during the Great Recession. That put everything we wanted to do on hold. Both of us were broke, with bills piling up on the kitchen counter after I got laid off from my part-time job as a substitute English teacher at Garfield High School. We were on food stamps and got our clothes from Goodwill. I tried to console her, first with kisses, then caresses, and before the night was over we had roof-raising sex. Afterwards, and for the thousandth time, I came close to proposing that we get married. But I had a failure of nerve, afraid she'd temporize or say no, or that because we were so poor we needed to wait. To be honest, I was never sure if she saw me as Mr. Right or just as Mr. Right Now.

So what I said to her that night, as we lay awake in each other's arms, our fingers intertwined, was getting fired might just be the change in luck we were looking for. Frances was so busy with customers, she didn't have time to change the locks. Or the code for the ADT alarm system. Naturally, Ieesha, who'd never stolen anything in her life, was reluctant, but I kept after her until she agreed.

Finally, after a few minutes, she enters the density of the storeroom's sooty darkness, her arms outstretched and feeling her way cat-footed. Among cardboard boxes of skin creams, conditioners, balms, and oils, she locates the holy grail of hair in three pea-green duffel bags stacked against the wall, like rugs rolled up for storage. She drags a chair beneath the storeroom window, then starts tossing the bags into the alley. As planned, I'm waiting outside, her old Toyota Corolla dappled with rust idling behind me. I catch each bag as it comes through the window, and throw them onto the backseat. The bags, I discover, weigh next to nothing. Yet for some reason, these sacks of something as common and plentiful as old hair are worth a lot of bank, why I don't know. Or why women struggling to pay their rent, poor women forced to choose between food and their winter fuel bill, go into debt shelling out between $1,000 and $3,000, and sometimes as much as $5,000, for a weave with real human hair. It baffled me until I read how some people must feel used things possess special properties. For example, someone on eBay bought Britney Spears's used gum for $14,000; someone else paid $115,000 for a handful of hair from Elvis Presley's pompadour, and his soiled, jockey-style shorts went on sale in September 2012 for $16,000 at an auction in England. (No one, by the way, bought his unwashed skivvies.) Another person spent $3,000 for Justin Timberlake's half-eaten French toast. So I guess some of those eBay buyers feel closer to the person they admire, maybe even with something of their essence magically clinging to the part they purchased.

As soon as Ieesha slides onto the passenger seat, pulling off her ski mask and drawing short, hard breaths as if she's been running up stairs, my foot lightly applies pressure to the gas pedal and I head for the freeway, my elbow out the window, my fingers curled on the roof of the car. Within fifteen minutes, we're back at our place. I park the car, we sling the bags over our shoulders, carry them inside to our first-floor unit, and stack them on the floor between the kitchenette and the sofa bed we sleep on. Ieesha sits down on a bedsheet still twisted from the night before when we were joined at the groin, knocking off her shoes run down at the heel and rubbing her ankles. She pulls a couple of wigs and a handful of hair extensions from one of the bags. She spreads them on our coffee table, frowning, then sits with her shoulders pulled in as if waiting for the ceiling to cave in.

"We're gonna be OK," I say.

"I don't know." Her voice is soft, sinus-clogged. "Tyrone, I don't feel good about this. I can't stop shaking. We're *not* burglars."

"We are now." I open a bottle of Bordeaux we've been saving to celebrate, filling up our only wineglass for her, and a large jam-jar for myself. I sit down beside her and pick up one of the wigs. Its texture between my fingertips is fluffy. I say, "You can blame Frances. She should have stood up for you. She *owes* you. What we need to do now is think about our next step. Where we can sell this stuff." Her head twitches back in reflex when I reach for one of the wigs and put it on her head, just out of curiosity, you know. Reluctantly, she lets me place it there, and I ask, "What's that feel like? A stocking cap? Is it hot?"

"I don't know. It feels . . ."

She never tells me how it feels.

So I ask another question. "What makes this hair so special? Where does it come from?"

Hands folded in her lap, she sits quietly and, for an instant, the wig that pools her face with obsidian tresses makes her look like someone I don't know. All of a sudden, I'm not sure what she might do next, but what she *does* do, after clearing her throat, is give me the hair-raising history and odyssey behind the property we've stolen. The bags, she says, come from a Buddhist temple near New Delhi, where young women shave their heads in an ancient ceremony of sacrifice called taking *pabbajja*. They give it up in order to renounce all vanity, and this letting go of things cosmetic and the chimera called the ego was their first step as nuns on a path to realizing that the essence of everything is emptiness. The hair ceremony was one of 84,000 Dharma gates. On the day their heads were shaved, they kneeled in their plain saris, there in the temple naos, and took 240 vows, the first five of which were no killing, no lying, no stealing, no sexual misconduct, and no drinking of alcohol. They didn't care what happened to their hair after the ceremony. Didn't know it would be sewn, stitched, and stapled onto the scalps of other people. But

Korean merchants were there. They paid the temple's abbot $10 for each head of fibrous protein. After that, the merchants, who controlled this commerce as tightly as the mafia did gambling, washed the hair clean of lice. From India, where these women cultivated an outward life of simplicity and an inward life free from illusion, the merchants transported their discarded, dead hair halfway around the planet where, ironically, it was cannibalized as commerce in a $9 billion industry for hair extensions devoted precisely to keeping women forever enslaved to the eyes of others.

As she explained all this, Ieesha leaves her wine untasted, and I don't say anything because my brain is stuttering, stalling on the unsyllabled thought that if you tug on a single, thin strand of hair, which has a life span of five and half years, you find it raddled to the rest of the world. I didn't see any of that coming until it arrived. I lift the jar of wine straight to my lips, empty it, and set it down with a click on the coffee table. When I look back at Ieesha, I realize she's smiling into one cheek as if remembering a delicious secret she can't share with me. That makes me down a second jar of Bordeaux. Then a third. I wonder, does the wig she's wearing itch or tingle? Does it feel like touching Justin Timberlake's unfinished French toast? Now the wine bottle is empty. We've got nothing on the empty racks of the refrigerator but a six-pack of beer, so I rise from the sofa to get that, a little woozy on my feet, careening sideways toward the kitchenette, but my full bladder redirects me toward the cubicle that houses our shower and toilet. I click on the light, close the door, and brace myself with one hand pressed against the wall. Standing there for a few minutes, my eyes closed, I feel rather than hear a police siren, and our smoke alarm. My stomach clenches.

Coming out of the bathroom, I find the wig she was wearing and the weaves that were on the coffee table burning in a wastebasket. Ieesha stands in the middle of the room, her cellphone pressed against her ear.

"What are you doing?" Smoke is stinging my eyes. "Who are you talking to?"

Her eyes are quiet. Everything about her seems quiet when she says, "Nine-one-one."

"*Why?*"

"Because it's the right thing to do."

I stare at her in wonder. She's offered us up, the way the women did their hair at the temple in New Delhi. I rush to draw water from the kitchen sink to put out the fire. I start throwing open the windows as there comes a loud knock, then pounding at the door behind me, but I can't take my eyes off her. She looks vulnerable but not weak, free, and more than enough for herself. I hear the wood of the door breaking, but as if from a great distance because suddenly I know, and she knows, that I understand. She's letting go all of it—the inheritance of hurt, the artificial and the inauthentic, the absurdities of color and caste stained at their roots by vanity and bondage to the body—and in this evanescent moment, when even I suddenly feel as if a weight has been lifted off my shoulders, she has never looked more beautiful and spiritually centered to me. There's shouting in the room now. Rough hands throw me facedown on the floor. My wrists are cuffed behind my back. Someone is reciting my Miranda rights. Then I feel myself being lifted to my feet. But I stop midway, resting on my right knee, my voice shaky as I look up at Ieesha, and say:

"Will you marry me?"

Two policemen lead her toward the shattered door, our first steps toward that American monastery called prison. She half turns, smiling, looking back at me, and her head nods: *Yes, yes, yes.*

"The Dharma and the Artist's Eye": Published in *International Review of African American Art*, vol. 21, no. 3, fall 2007. "Dharma for a Dangerous Time": Published in *Shambhala Sun*, September 2006. "The Dharma of Social Transformation": Published in *Tricycle: The Buddhist Review*, winter 2006. "Be Peace Embodied": Published in *Shambhala Sun*, July 2004. "The King We Need: Teachings for a Nation in Search of Itself": Published in *Shambhala Sun*, January 2005. "Why Buddhists Should Vote": Published in *Tricycle: The Buddhist Review*, fall 2000. "Is Mine Bigger Than Yours?": Published in *Buddhadharma*, winter 2010. "Why Buddhism for Black America Now?": A paper presented at West Chester University's Buddhist Ethics Symposium, November 19, 2010. "Mindfulness and the Beloved Community": Published in *Turning Wheel: Socially Engaged Buddhism*, summer 2003. "The Meaning of Barack Obama": Published in *Shambhala Sun*, November 2008. "Every Twenty-Eight Hours: The Case of Trayvon Martin": Published online on the website of *Tricycle: The Buddhist Review;* Tricycle.com; "Every 28 Hours: The Case of Trayvon Martin," blog entry by Charles Johnson, June 18, 2013. "A Full-Bodied Zen": Published in *Buddhadharma*, winter 2004. "Going Beyond Ethnic Dualism": Published in *Tricycle: The Buddhist Review*, summer 2001. "Foreword for *Nixon under the Bodhi Tree and Other Works of Buddhist Fiction*": Published in *Nixon under the Bodhi Tree and Other Works of Buddhist Fiction*, edited by Kate Wheeler, 2004. "Introduction for *Why Is American Buddhism So White?*": Published in *Buddhadharma*, winter 2011. "We Think, Therefore We Are": Published in *Shambhala Sun*, May 2008. "Prince of the Ascetics": Published in *Shambhala Sun*, January 2008. "The Cynic": Published in *Boston Review*, November–December 2007. "Kamadhatu, a Modern Sutra": Published in *Shambhala Sun*, March 2012. "Welcome to Wedgwood": Published in *Shambhala Sun*, March 2011. "Guinea Pig": Published in *Boston Review*, January–February 2011. "The Weave": Published in *The Iowa Review*, fall 2014.